A Career in Law
THE WAY IN

3rd Edition

Brian Heap
Director
Higher Education Advice and
Planning Service

HLT Publications

HLT PUBLICATIONS
200 Greyhound Road, London W14 9RY

First Published 1990
Revised Edition 1991
Third Edition 1992

ISBN 0 7510 0225 9

British Library Cataloguing-in-Publication.

A CIP Catalogue record for this book is available from the
British Library.

Printed and bound in Great Britain.

CONTENTS

ACKNOWLEDGEMENTS

I would like to thank UCCA/PCAS for advising me on their application systems. I am also grateful for the assistance of the Department of Education and Science for providing up-to-date details of graduate employment.

Brian Heap

NB Higher education in the UK is being completely reorganised. The new Further and Higher Education Act will among other things allow polytechnics to change their names to universities.

At the time of publication, however, no official name changes have been authorised. Students applying for places from September 1992 for entry in 1993 will continue to apply to 'polytechnics' and they will appear thus in the PCAS Handbook 1992.

ACKNOWLEDGEMENTS

1   INTRODUCTION

'Law is the cement of society and also an essential medium of change. A knowledge of law increases one's understanding of public affairs. Its study promotes accuracy of expression, facility in argument and skill in interpreting the written word, as well as some understanding of social values. Its practice does, of course, call for much routine, careful and unexciting work and it is for you to decide whether you think you are temperamentally suited to it.'

This extract is taken from that excellent little book *Learning the Law* by Glanville Williams (Stevens and Sons) which should be essential reading for anyone contemplating the study of Law at a university, polytechnic or college or as a professional qualification.

No law case, however, can ever proceed without very careful preparation and similarly no student should ever make the decision to follow such a demanding course of study – or any course of study – without being fully aware of what is involved and without careful planning.

At a recent interview for a place in Law at Oxford, one applicant proclaimed that he had wanted to be a lawyer since he was eight years of age! There may have been other reasons for his rejection, but an opinion concerning a career in law as seen on TV, with a clever criminal lawyer manipulating a jury, is no more a true reflection of the extent of the career than the work of a brain or heart surgeon is to a career in medicine.

No solicitor or barrister would ever jump to conclusions on the basis of superficial evidence and no intending law student should be attracted to the career simply because of its status and high salaries, as is often the case. Let us be equally professional therefore and proceed to explore what a career in law really involves, what courses are available and how to prepare a successful application.

2   STUDYING LAW

Studying law not only provides a means of entering the legal profession, but is also a stimulating and rewarding academic exercise. The development of logical thought and methodical preparation of argument is something that is of value in any career that you may choose to follow.

As a lawyer, you will need to master the detail of the law, together with the ability to present this knowledge in a rational and decisive way.

In addition to acquiring a general knowledge of the English Legal System, the student will also study what are known as the 'core subjects'. These are Constitutional Law, Contract Law, Criminal Law, Tort, Land Law and the Law of Trusts. Most institutions allow students to supplement these basic subjects with additional options in a variety of other legal specialities. However, do remember that if you are intending to go on to become a barrister or a solicitor you must ensure that you do cover these 'core subjects' to keep your qualifying period to a minimum.

Sources of English Law

England is a democracy, and as such depends heavily upon Parliament for the creation of law. However, England is also a common law jurisdiction, which means that many legal principles are found by reference to earlier cases. Our membership of the European Community has also introduced aspects of EC law into our legal system and a knowledge of this area of law is essential.

Your studies will familiarise you with the techniques necessary to interpret legislation, ascertain the essential principles in a case, and discover the applicability of European law.

Statutory Interpretation

The traditional view that Parliament is sovereign, and can therefore legislate as it sees fit is subject now to the effect of EC law. Nevertheless, Parliament may make new laws, bringing about great political and social changes, and it may alter, simplify, or improve or repeal existing laws. The judge must apply the law made by Parliament; he is not free to ignore or alter it. In order to apply the law, he must interpret the statute. In doing this he will adopt one of a number of approaches; namely the literal rule, the golden rule and the mischief rule or purposive approach.

The literal rule requires the judge to give the words in the statute their literal meaning even if the result is undesirable. If, however, the result becomes manifestly absurd or repugnant, the judge may vary the meaning of the words to avoid the absurdity or repugnance. This is called the golden rule.

In most cases, though, the words of a statute are capable of bearing more than one meaning, and the judge must then decide which meaning Parliament intended. To assist him, he will use the mischief rule or purposive approach, which requires him to consider what mischief or defect Parliament was trying to correct, or what purpose the statute was designed to serve.

In addition there are grammatical rules of construction (all with impossible latin names!) and presumptions to assist in ascertaining the meaning of words in a statute.

Judicial Precedent

As well as being confined by statute law, the judge must also follow certain earlier judicial decisions. This doctrine of binding judicial precedent, or s*tare decisis,* is vital to an understanding of the law. It should ensure that there is certainty, uniformity and consistency. It can, however, lead to inflexibility and injustice.

In the course of your studies you will develop the ability to define the essential binding part of the judgment, called the *ratio decidendi.* The rest of the judgment is termed *obiter dicta* and may be used as guidance in the future. It is possible to avoid being bound by an earlier decision if one can distinguish the facts of the case from that which fails to be considered. You must, however, be careful not to 'distinguish the indistinguishable'!

Civil and Criminal Law

The English legal system makes a distinction between civil and criminal law. The criminal law is concerned with wrongs that not only affect 'the victim' but which are of a nature that society has an interest in preventing and punishing them. The civil law is also concerned with wrongs, but the nature of the wrong is such that it is left to the aggrieved individual to bring an action. We sometimes refer to the civil law as being a way of recognising rights.

In criminal cases we talk of a prosecution being taken against the defendant, and the result of the case is referred to as a conviction or acquittal. If there is a conviction the defendant will be punished for example by a fine or imprisonment. Whereas in civil cases the person who institutes the action, or sues, is referred to as the plaintiff, and the person against whom the action lies is referred to as the defendant. The result of a civil case is called judgment for the plaintiff or defendant, and usually compensation is awarded.

Civil and criminal cases take place in different courts and different procedural rules apply. Cases in civil courts are known by the names of the parties: *Smith* v *Bloggs* (pronounced Smith and Bloggs). In criminal cases the prosecution is usually brought in the name of the Queen, and would be written as *Reg.* or *R* v *Smith* (pronounced as the Queen against Smith, or informally R v Smith).

The Court Structure

The distinction between civil and criminal law is reflected in the court structure. While several courts have jurisdiction over both civil and criminal cases, civil cases are dealt with by a different system of courts dealing with criminal cases. What follows is a basic outline of the two court structures.

Civil court structure

The Magistrates' and County courts are at the entry level to the civil system, along with a number of specialist tribunals eg Social Security Appeals, Industrial and Rent Tribunals. At the next level are the Crown Court (in its civil jurisdiction) and the Employment Appeals Tribunal. Above is the High Court which has three main divisions: Family; Queen's Bench (including the Admiralty and Commercial Courts); and Chancery. The Court of Appeal (Civil Division) is the first appellate court; the second – and highest – appellate court for civil cases is the House of Lords.

Criminal court structure

The Magistrates' Courts are the starting point for all criminal cases, and on the next tier is the Crown Court. The Queen's Bench Divisional Court hears appeals from the Magistrates' Courts, both direct and via the Crown Court. The Criminal Division of the Court of Appeal comes next in the hierarchy and again the House of Lords is the final appellate court.

Role of the European Court of Justice

Any court may refer a point of European law to the European Court of Justice for decision (this is not an appeal).

Personnel of the Law

The judges that preside over the courts are selected from the ranks of practising lawyers. The higher the court, the more senior the judge. The Lord Chancellor is responsible for advising the Government and the Queen on the appointment of judges.

The judges of the House of Lords are called Lords of Appeal in Ordinary, and judges in the Court of Appeal are called Lord Justices of Appeal. High Court judges are referred to as puisne (pronounced 'puny', and from the old French for 'junior' or 'inferior') judges, whilst circuit judges sit in the County Courts and Crown Court.

In the Magistrates' Court decisions are made by lay people, called Justices of the Peace, or by a stipendiary magistrate who is legally qualified. The professional lawyers who present cases in court are usually barristers, although cases in the lower courts may be presented by solicitors. Solicitors tend to give general advice and assistance to their clients, referring cases to barristers for more specialist advice and advocacy.

3   A CAREER AS A SOLICITOR (ENGLAND AND WALES)

At the present time there are about 50,000 solicitors in practice in the UK (compared with 6,000 barristers, 2,000 judges and 29,000 magistrates). The great majority of solicitors work in private practice with about 5,000 being employed by commercial and industrial organisations and 3,000 in local government work.

A solicitor in private practice usually starts as an assistant solicitor, later becoming a partner and sharing the profits and management of the business. Firms of solicitors vary from large partnerships in the City of London and other large towns to smaller 'High Street' practices throughout England and Wales.

Private Practice

The role of the solicitor in practice is to give legal advice and to counsel their clients on the best way to proceed with their particular problem. Much of the work is quite routine in nature and articled clerks or other clerks (legal executives) often assist in these duties.

A large proportion of a 'High Street' solicitor's work will be involved with conveyancing property – the purchase of houses, flats, shops, even factories! Anyone purchasing property needs to have safeguards against any future plans for the development or otherwise of the land on which the property is situated and also needs advice on the contract of sale, etc.

Solicitors also advise clients on the course of action to take if they are facing criminal charges – anything in fact from a traffic offence to murder – since many such cases need to be defended in a court of law.

The drafting of wills is yet another side of the solicitor's work and he or she may also be responsible to see that the terms of the will are executed (by acting as an executor or administrator). Compensation claims, divorce, custody of children, and maintenance also falls within the province of the law in addition to anything from the setting up of companies to debt collecting.

In small town practices, many clients will use the same firm throughout their lives, but at the other end of the spectrum large city practices may concentrate on one particular specialism such as company law, shipping, airline or commercial law, or libel and slander (defamation).

If you have a hidden talent, therefore, for drafting important documents then there could be a place for you; alternatively as a solicitor you might prefer court work (litigation), conducting cases in magistrates' or county courts.

Civil Service

Outside private practice there are still very many opportunities to practise law – the Civil Service being one of them.

Large numbers of lawyers (solicitors and barristers) work for the government legal service in almost all departments. Civil Service departments are constantly needing to review their policies (economic and political) and legal experts are in constant demand. These departments include:

Agriculture, Fisheries and Food which includes the EC common agricultural policy;

Education and Science – from nursery school to universities – involving pay scales, the youth service and schools meals service;

Energy – coal, gas, oil, electricity and nuclear power;

Employment – covering all aspects of manpower;

Environmental and Transport – involving housing, planning, road construction and transport;

Health and Social Security – administering the National Health Services;

Trade and Industry – EC policy, exports and imports;

The Ministry of Defence – formulating defence policy and administering the armed services.

There are also other departments such as HM Treasury (economic policy); the Cabinet Office (administering Cabinet business); the Central Office of Information; the Foreign and Commonwealth Office (British interests abroad) and the Home Office (law and order and justice). Another important legal area is that of the Lord Chancellor's Department which administers all criminal and civil courts (except magistrates' courts) in England and Wales.

Other departments include the Land Registry, Inland Revenue, the Office of Fair Trading, the Health and Safety Executive, HM Customs and Excise, the Crown Estate Office, the Charity Commission, the Department of Public Prosecutions, the Public Record Office, Ordnance Survey, National Savings and Stationery Office.

There are, however, other opportunities for work as a solicitor, for example in local government within departments of education, town and country planning, and social services. In such a role much of your time will be spent arranging for the election of council members to carry out their duties.

Alternatively, you may be amongst the 5,000 solicitors in commerce or industry since most large companies now have their own legal departments dealing with business law, company law, taxation and other specialised areas.

Have You the Right Qualities to be a Solicitor?

A recent report from the Law Society stated that:

'The Dickensian image of a solicitor as a middle-class, elderly man has changed quite considerably. Solicitors these days come from both sexes, all races, and from any social background. The profession is "getting younger" too – about half of all practising solicitors these days are under 36 and only a minority of solicitors qualifying now have family connections with the legal profession. It is no coincidence that many well-known figures have made it to the very top in government, commerce and industry after qualifying as solicitors.'

But what qualities do you need?

a)   Have you a good memory?
b)   Are you numerate?
c)   Have you a good command of language?
d)   Have you the ability to get to grips with a problem?
e)   Have you high personal standards of integrity?
f)   Have you the ability to communicate with others at all levels – and to listen to them?
g)   Have you the patience to cope with routine matters?
h)   Have you a cool head when the pressure is on?
i)   Have you common sense?

Qualifying to be a Solicitor

The majority of newly qualified solicitors have taken a degree in law or another subject and this is the recommended route.

Law Graduates

One advantage in taking a law degree is that the total period of training will be shorter than for those taking a non-law degree.

Following your law degree you will then take a one year Finals course. Details of courses are available from College of Law, Braboeuf Manor, St Catherine's, Portsmouth Road, Guildford GU3 1HA. Courses are also offered at the following polytechnics: Birmingham, Bristol, City of London, Leeds, Manchester, Newcastle, Nottingham and Wolverhampton. The course is then followed by two years as an articled clerk.

Non-law Graduates

After taking your degree – in any subject – you need to apply (well in advance) for a place on the one year Common Professional Examination (CPE) course. These courses are offered at the College of Law (above) or at one of the polytechnics (above) or at Leicester or Wales Polytechnics who also prepare students for this examination. After the CPE examination, you will then be required to take the Law Society's Final

7

Examination. Following this examination you will then serve two years as an articled clerk.

Mature Students

Some people decide to train as a solicitor at a later stage in their careers. To do so you must be over 25 years of age to enrol with the Law Society. You will need to satisfy the Society that a minimum standard of education has been attained and that you can show exceptional ability in business, academic, professional or administrative work. Like non-law graduates the Common Professional Examination must be taken, but over a two year (not a one year) period. The Law Society's Final Examination must also be passed and then you will serve two years training as an articled clerk. (Students or others working in the legal profession may gain exemptions from some of the examinations to be taken.)

School Leavers (very few pupils decide to qualify in this way)

All school leavers must first apply to the Law Society for an enrolment certificate and they must have achieved a minimum standard of education. The requirements are:

a)   Four GCE passes or GCSE (Grades A, B or C), including three 'A' Levels; or
b)   Five GCE passes or GCSE (Grades A, B or C), including two 'A' Levels; or
c)   Six GCE passes or GCSE (Grades A, B or C), including two 'A' Levels and two 'AS' Levels.

There is also a minimum points system in operation. The table below should be used to calculate the points required at 'A' Level and 'AS' Level.

GRADE	'A' LEVEL POINTS	'AS' LEVEL POINTS
A	10	5
B	8	4
C	6	3
D	4	2
E	2	1

The minimum points required are as follows:

14 points from two 'A' Level subjects taken at one sitting.

18 points from three 'A' Level subjects or two 'A' Level and two 'AS' Level subjects taken at one sitting.

20 points from three 'A' Level or two 'A' Level and two 'AS' Level subjects taken at not more than two sittings.

('AS' Level subjects may not be taken into account when calculating points unless a minimum of two 'A' Levels is held. Equivalent qualifications will be considered in lieu of the above.)

School leavers then take a one year course at a polytechnic in four law subjects in the first half of an examination known as the Solicitors' First Examination. (Only a limited number of places is available for this examination.)

Five years must then be spent as an articled clerk. During this time, part time study must be done for a further four law subjects, making up the second half of the Solicitors' First Examination (it is usual for two subjects to be taken after the first year and two after the second).

After completing the Solicitor's First Examination, you must attend a one year course studying for the Law Society's Final Examination, but the time you spend on the course will count as part of your training as an articled clerk. When you have completed your training in articles and you have passed the final exams, you may be admitted as a solicitor.

The following details are taken from the Law Society's booklet *Solicitors – a Career in Law.*

The Solicitors' Final Examination

All solicitors have to pass the Final Examination in order to qualify. Guildford may be the best known of the colleges, probably because the administrative head offices of the College of Law are located there. But you should note that the courses at Chester, London and in the relevant polytechnics are on an entirely equal footing with the Guildford course, and will not affect your acceptance as an articled clerk. A student at, for example, Bristol University may well find it more convenient to stay on in the same accommodation and take his or her Finals at Bristol Polytechnic. The subjects studied on the Finals Course are a mix of the theoretical and the practical, concentrating on the basic spread of work done in a solicitor's office. They are:

a)   Accounts;
b)   Business organisations and insolvency, employment law and consumer protection;
c)   Conveyancing, wills, probate and administration, family law;
d)   Litigation; and revenue law, which is taught within (b) and (c).

Some subjects will have been covered (possibly as an option) as part of the law degree, though inevitably with different emphasis; others will present for the first time the sharp end of decision making as a solicitor.

Articles

The time you spend 'in articles' as a trainee solicitor is your opportunity to put into practice your hard won theoretical knowledge. You will learn about the day-to-day running of the business, and how to deal with clients, whilst gradually increasing the scope and responsibility of your work.

9

There are many different types of articles available – in local government, magistrates' courts, industry and commerce etc – but the majority of students take articles in private practice. Finding articles is your own responsibility; vacancies are advertised widely in various publications, and you will find lists of suitable firms in ROSET (Register of Solicitors Employing Trainees), which can be purchased from the Law Society if your college does not have a copy. You can also obtain help from the Law Society's Appointments Register, from local law societies and of course from careers advisers. You might have to attend several interviews before finding the firm which is right for you. However, you will find more and more firms operating the 'milk round' by visiting universities and colleges in order to interview students.

The type of training you receive will depend very much upon the nature of the firm you join. A large commercial firm will offer a different kind of training from a small practice, and if you join a specialist firm you will inevitably receive a rather specialised training.

It is up to you to balance the pros and cons. Your period in articles is fundamental in shaping your career, so wherever you apply, try to talk to the people you may be working with during the first two years of your articles to get a 'feel' for the firm and whether you will do well there. You will have to cover at least three out of eight broad areas of law during your articles, monitoring your own progress by keeping a diary or checklist of tasks performed and topics covered. You will also have to attend a Supplementary Accounts Course during your articles – and, of course, you should go to any other seminars or courses which might be useful to you.

Ultimately, it will be up to you to make sure that your training satisfies the Law Society's requirements. Once you have successfully applied to be admitted to the Roll of Solicitors, your employers may well invite you to stay on with them – although, of course, you are not obliged to accept the offer if you prefer to go elsewhere.

Further Reading

A Career in Law, BA Hogan, Sweet and Maxwell (1981).
Before you see a Solicitor, Gerald Sanctuary, Oyez Publishing (1983).
How to Study Law, A Bradney, V Fisher and others, Sweet and Maxwell (1986).
Learning the Law, Glanville Williams, Stevens (1945: 11th edition 1982).
Which Firm of Solicitors?, John Pritchard, Legalease Limited (1987).

Further details can be obtained from the Law Society (address all enquiries to 'Careers Information'), 113 Chancery Lane, London WC2A 1PL.

4   A CAREER AS A BARRISTER

Although changes are now taking place within the legal profession, barristers have traditionally been regarded as 'specialists' who work through solicitors in the same way that medical consultants work through general practitioners. In this way the solicitor consults barristers on aspects of the law in the case of complex legal issues and the latter will appear in court on behalf of solicitors' clients.

Such cases will initially be prepared by the solicitor, after which the barrister will be required to undertake a considerable amount of detailed research before presenting his client's case in court. The knowledge required in some specialisations is quite considerable and those barristers specialising in patent work often have science or engineering degrees.

Most barristers will specialise, the main alternatives being in common law (family law, crime, divorce, etc.) or chancery (company law, tax, property, trust or estates work). In either case barristers usually specialise in one of these branches, particularly in London.

All barristers, however, do not necessarily spend most of their time in court. Much depends on the type of specialisation they follow. Common law barristers will undoubtedly be involved in court work; those working in chancery, however, will not.

The Bar is a relatively small profession with approximately 6,000 in practice, at least 75 per cent of them in London. Barristers share chambers and the services of barristers' clerks and since they are not permitted to set up in practice on their own on completion of their pupillage, they are required to find a 'seat' in chambers. Once in chambers, however, they are in effect 'self-employed' and are dependent on solicitors offering them work, through their clerks in chambers.

After 15 years of experience at the Bar, a barrister can apply to the Lord Chancellor for a patent as a Queen's Counsel (taking silk). It is necessary to take silk in order to become a high court judge.

Barristers' Clerks should also be mentioned here since they occupy an important place in the lives of any barrister. A senior clerk and the juniors working with him service all the barristers in one set of chambers. They act as an intermediary between solicitors and barristers, decide which cases their barristers will accept and decide which barrister in their chambers will deal with a case and fix the fee. They will also arrange the times when the case will be heard and subsequently receive a percentage of each barrister's fees. In consequence their income can be very high (sometimes more than the barrister!). Recruitment is open to school leavers with a good educational background. Competition is considerable and training is mainly 'on the job'.

Skills

The following skills have been identified as relevant to barristers and will be taught to students as part of the vocational course: Legal Research, Fact Management, Opinion Writing, Interviewing, Negotiating, Drafting and Advocacy.

Initially, in order to prepare students for the discrete areas of skills training, there will be short courses in Communication Skills, Writing Skills for the Barrister and Numeracy.

Students will learn these skills mainly by gaining experience of them in dealing with realistic sets of case papers. A central part of the learning process will be role play and students will be encouraged to make full use of the equipment for videoing performances in their roles. Students will be called upon to interview one another, role playing both lay and professional clients; to negotiate solutions to legal problems with one another, to draft documents and pleadings as required; to role play the conduct of cases in courts and tribunals both as barristers and as others in the trial process; to carry out legal research using original source materials and practitioners' works; to write opinions on the merits of a case and on the evidence, and to experience how to develop and present a theory of the case and find a solution to the problem presented.

Have You the Right Qualities to be a Barrister?

a)   Would you enjoy doing very detailed research into a subject?
b)   Would you enjoy unravelling the legal intricacies of a subject?
c)   Would you enjoy being able to learn about and then speak knowledgeably on the most technical aspects of a subject and even examine an expert witness?
d)   Could you stand up in front of your class and explain a very obscure subject so that the rest of the class could understand it?

Qualifying to be a Barrister

The process of training to become a practising barrister in England and Wales is divided into three stages which must be completed in the following order.

The Academic Stage

This stage is completed by studying Law or a combination of Law and another subject at degree level, or alternatively it is possible to study any subject to degree level which is then followed by a special one year Common Professional Examination (CPE) course at either City University or Central London Polytechnic. The third route is to be accepted by an Inn of Court as a non-graduate mature student and then follow a two year CPE course at the polytechnics at Bristol, Manchester, Newcastle or Central London. There are four Inns of Court – Lincoln's Inn, Inner Temple, Middle Temple or Gray's Inn – all in London. Prospective entrants to the Bar must be admitted as student members of one of the Inns of Court – the minimum entry requirement being a first degree with at least second class honours.

The Vocational Stage

The method of completing this stage of training varies according to whether a student does or does not intend to practise as a Member of the Bar of England and Wales or the Channel Islands, or in the territory of any Member State of the European Community.

Those wishing to practise must attend the full time course at the Inns of Court School of Law and satisfactorily complete all the tests, assessments and examinations set as part of that course.

A student who does not intend to practise in England and Wales is required to complete the Vocational Stage by examination by entering and passing the Bar examination set for that purpose.

The Vocational Course aims to provide a practical training in the specialist skills required by barristers, and to ensure competence in those skills. This will be achieved through practice in the tasks most commonly performed by junior members of the Bar during the early years of practice and most particularly, in the second six months of pupillage. Approximately two thirds of class contact time in the course will be devoted to skills training, whilst no more than 40 per cent of all class contact time will be spent acquiring new knowledge. All aspects of the course will emphasise the need for a professional approach to work, and will encourage the students to develop a respect for the principles of professional conduct. The student's successful completion of the course will be assessed in the practical work, and in tests and examinations carried out during the year.

Courses in preparation for the Bar Examination are at present offered by various colleges including:

City of London Polytechnic
Faculty of Law
84 Moorgate
London EC2M 6SQ

Holborn College
200 Greyhound Road
London W14 9RY

West London Polytechnic
School of Law and Social Science
St Mary's Road
Ealing
London W5 5RF

Manchester Polytechnic
Department of Law
John Dalton Building
Chester Street
Manchester M1 5GD

South Bank Polytechnic
Department of Law and Government
Faculty of Management and Policy Studies
103 Borough Road,
London SE1 0AA

Polytechnic of Central London
Faculty of Law
Red Lion Square
London WC1R 4SR

Students should note that all institutions offering courses in preparation for the Bar Examination are independent of the CLE, and have sole control over admissions to their courses and the discipline of students attending them. Students should apply direct to the institutions for information on course dates, fees and registration procedures.

Pupillage

This is a twelve month period of apprenticeship which is, in general, served with one or more practising barristers.

On successful completion of this third stage of training a barrister is qualified to enter practice.

Full details of training as a barrister are available from the Council of Legal Education, 4 Gray's Inn Place, London WC1R 5DX.

5 CHOOSING A DEGREE COURSE

Non-Law Degree Courses

Choosing a degree course will depend on several factors, and one of these must be the motivation and interest to be able to pursue a subject for the next three years.

Some students are ready to make career decisions at 17 or 18 and choose degree courses leading to specific career areas such as law, business studies, surveying, architecture, etc. Others, however, are not sure, and they may turn to their 'A' Level subjects as a basis for future studies.

Whatever the degree subject, the level of degree course to be followed initially is that of the Bachelor or first degree which is offered by universities, polytechnics, colleges of higher education (not to be confused with colleges of further education, which offer courses for boys and girls at 16, as an alternative to staying on at school), institutes of higher education and specialist colleges, eg colleges of agriculture, art, etc. The exception to this rule concerns some Scottish universities in which the first degree is a Master of Arts degree (MA) awarded to students in the Scottish system who usually start their courses one year earlier than students at English and Welsh universities. These MA courses normally last four years. An MA in Scotland is equivalent to a BA in English and Welsh universities. The most well known Bachelor degrees are BA and BSc (Bachelor of Arts and Sciences). There are others, however, such as the LLB (Bachelor of Laws), MB (Bachelor of Medicine), B Eng (Engineering), B Ed (Education), B Mus (Music), B Tech (Technology). All these degrees are equivalent to each other.

Honours degrees are divided into 'classes' – 1st, 2nd (sub-divided into 2:1 and 2:2) and 3rd. Ordinary and Pass degrees are awarded to those who fail some exams on the 'Honours' course.

Types of Degree Course

There are six types of courses:

a) *Single Honours courses* This is a study of one subject, although at some universities and polytechnics it may be possible to study other subsidiary subjects for part of the course.

b) *Joint Honours courses* These courses involve the study of two subjects. These subjects might have similarities, eg Mathematics and Computer Science, or French and Italian, or they might be quite different, eg Geography and Music. It is worth noting that there may be fewer places on these courses and higher standards of entry may be required.

c) *Combined Honours courses* These courses usually involve the study of several subjects, eg the Combined courses at Leicester and Newcastle Universities and the General Honours course at Birmingham University.

d) *Sandwich courses* These courses consist of periods of work experience which are combined with theoretical study at university, polytechnic or college. Experience with firms and other organisations can be a great asset to the student who may often be offered a job with the firm at the end of his or her degree course. (Sandwich courses in Law are offered by Brunel University and the polytechnics at Bristol, Bournemouth, Nottingham and Sheffield.) The thick sandwich course usually concerns those sixth formers who have managed to obtain a sponsorship. On leaving school, students usually spend a year with their firm on full pay. This is followed by three years at university, returning to the firm in the fifth year.

e) *External Degree courses* 'External' degrees are awarded on satisfactory completion of the prescribed examinations by the University of London to students who have prepared themselves for the examinations on full-time or part-time courses at colleges outside the University of London's Federation of Colleges or by distance learning courses or independent private study. These degrees have exactly the same standing as degrees obtained by full-time study at universities, polytechnics and colleges of higher education. A number of colleges offer courses leading to University of London external degrees and Holborn College, one of the largest independent colleges of law in the United Kingdom and an Associate College of Wolverhampton Polytechnic offers courses leading to the University of London external LLB (Honours) degree in Law and BSc (Economics) degrees in Accountancy, Management Studies or Economics and Management Studies.

f) *Franchised Degree Courses* As higher education evolves in the 90s flexibility is the key to many of the new courses. Many institutions are franchising their courses at various levels to other institutions in the United Kingdom and overseas.

In October 1990 Holborn College in London was validated by the CNAA to take a franchise of the LLB (Honours) Degree from Wolverhampton Polytechnic and is now an Associate College of the Polytechnic. This degree programme provides one of the widest selections of course options for an LLB (Honours) Degree available in the United Kingdom. Application has been made to the Department of Education and Science for award status for United Kingdom 'home students' at Holborn College and if this is granted it will amount to approximately £695 fees payment in addition to maintenance grants where applicable.

Holborn College also offers an LLB (Honours) Degree by distance learning with optional support tuition in conjunction with Wolverhampton Polytechnic which gives students total flexibility in the way in which they prepare for a law degree. Students may transfer between full-time, part-time and distance learning modes as personal circumstances change through the period of study.

Choosing a degree course other than Law could stem from considering 'A' Level subject options. In the first instance you could choose your favourite 'A' Level

16

subject or subjects (at least you have a good idea of what they involve). Talk to your tutors about a possible degree course in these subjects and read through prospectuses to obtain a better idea of the topics to be covered.

However, it is not just necessary to choose the 'A' Level subject you enjoy the most. Each 'A' Level subject is part of a larger family of similar subjects, and with your interest in other 'A' Level subjects there could be several obvious connections which will produce alternative ideas.

Let us take a look at some 'A' Level subjects and appropriate degree courses which would enable you to go on to train as a solicitor or barrister after graduation.

Arts and Humanities Subjects

Ancient History – Archaeology, Biblical Studies, Greek, Latin, Classical Studies, Religious Studies and Philosophy.

British Government and Politics – Economics, European Studies, History, Law, Public Administration, Strategic Studies.

Economics – Accountancy (Actuarial work), Banking, Business and Business Finance, Estate Management, Operational Research, Planning, Quantity Surveying, Social Studies.

English – Anglo-Saxon, Drama, European Literature, Journalism, Languages, Librarianship.

Geography – African, Asian and European Studies, Earth Sciences and Geology, Environmental Studies, Estate Management, Fisheries Management, Land Economy, Meteorology, Oceanography, Town and Country Planning.

History – American Studies, Anthropology, Biblical Studies, Law, History (covering various countries and continents of the world).

Languages – Apart from those languages being studied to 'A' Level it is also possible to start new languages from scratch on many university courses, eg Arabic, Chinese, Japanese, Scandinavian, East European, Near Eastern and Far Eastern languages.

Religious Studies – Archaeology, Education, History, Philosophy, Psychology, Social Administration.

Science Subjects

Biology – Agricultural and Animal Sciences, Biological Sciences, Dentistry, Dietetics, Ecology, Environmental Science, Forestry, Horticulture, Marine Biology, Medicine, Nursing, Nutrition, Occupational Therapy, Pharmacology, Pharmacy, Psychology, Speech Science, Veterinary Science, Zoology.

Chemistry – As above and also Biochemistry, Chemical Engineering, Colour Chemistry, Food Science, Fuel Science, Oil Technology, Textile Chemistry.

Geology – Geography, Mining and Mineral Exploitation, Mining Surveying.

Mathematics – Accountancy, Actuarial Science, Business Studies, Computer Science, Economics, Engineering, Operational Research.

Physics – Building and Building Services Engineering (Heating – Refrigeration – Acoustics), all engineering subjects, Materials Science, Naval Architecture.

Other Subjects

Having read through these lists you may form ideas about some course options but *beware*. Do not reject courses you have never heard of and do not assume you know very much about those courses you think are familiar! The following list will give you just a taste of what might be involved when choosing some subjects to study.

Agriculture – The choice may lie between the very practical type of farming courses or those which have a greater emphasis on agricultural science.

American Studies – This covers the history and literature of the USA (and including Canada at Birmingham University).

Archaeology – This usually involves a study of archaeology in the British Isles and the Mediterranean countries. These courses sometimes include Ancient History.

Art – Practical work courses are offered at some universities as well as at the polytechnics and colleges. The History of Art, Architecture or Design may also be studied; in some cases both practical and theoretical work is done on the same course.

Biology/Biochemistry – Choices include a bias towards Medicine, Nutrition, Agriculture, Pharmacology, Biotechnology, Marine, Plant, Fishery and Animal Sciences.

Business Studies – This is a very wide field (see *The Way In – Business and Management* (HLT Publications)) and covers accountancy and financial management, management services, marketing, sales, personnel work, retail management, textile management, estate management, and hotel management. In some universities, Business can be combined with a language, at Birmingham, Leeds, Loughborough, and in some polytechnics, at Birmingham, Kingston, Manchester, Sheffield and Nottingham. European Business Studies is an option in several polytechnics and colleges, at Lancashire, Humberside, Middlesex, Nottingham, Leeds Polytechnics and at Buckinghamshire College. London University's external degree in Management Studies or Economics and Management Studies (both BSc Econ) can be studied on a three year full term programme at Holborn College. It is also possible to take a one year London University Diploma in Economics at Holborn College and to transfer to the degree course at the end of the year. (Offers for all these courses are in the DD–EE range.)

Chemistry – Courses can be taken with one other subject in Year 1, eg at Bristol, Liverpool, Lancaster; or with a language, at Nottingham and East Anglia; or with a year in Europe or USA, at East Anglia, Surrey; or as sandwich courses, at Bath, Aston, Loughborough, Brunel.

Drama – There is a practical performance bias at Aberystwyth, East Anglia and Hull. (Dance is offered at Surrey, Birmingham and Bretton Hall College).

Environmental Science – This subject has an emphasis on Biology/Geography, at Bradford, Sheffield universities or with Chemistry/Geology, at Kent and Sussex, or with Physics, at Lancaster, or with Geography/Planning, at University College London or Sheffield (Poly), or a study of Environmental Health, at Salford, Leeds (Poly), and Thames (Poly).

Engineering – Many specialisations are offered, eg Electrical/Electronics (including telecommunications and systems), Chemical (including Nuclear, Fuel and Energy), Mechanical and Production, Civil and Structural Engineering.

French – Courses could have a bias toward literature, at some universities, such as Oxbridge and Durham, or alternatively as European Studies courses, at Surrey and Bath or Cardiff (European Community Studies).

History – Courses may offer a choice between British, European, Ancient, Medieval or Modern History or the History of the World, eg Newcastle (Russia and Latin America), or Warwick (Mexico and Cuba).

Materials Science – This is an ideal course for those with equal interests between Physics and Chemistry and leading to careers in metallurgy, polymers, glasses, ceramics. (There is a real shortage of graduates in this subject area.)

Mathematics – A choice is available from Pure Maths, Applied Maths, Statistics and Operational Research.

Psychology – This includes Social or Human Psychology, eg at Bradford and Loughborough, Educational Occupational and Clinical Psychology, at Bangor and Cardiff.

Religious Studies – This subject may cover the origins of Christianity, Islam, Judaism, Buddhism, but studies may also involve Biblical Studies and Theology.

Social Administration – This subject covers aspects of public administration, housing, health and mental illness and other similar topics.

Social Studies – Courses involve the nature and development of modern society (Economics, Politics, Sociology, Geography) and methods of social investigation.

Law Degree Courses

If you decide to choose a law degree course it is useful to start by understanding what qualities are sought by admissions tutors. Here are some quotations:

'We look for qualities of perseverance, a logical mind able to exclude the irrelevant, patience, and, ideally, common sense.'

'Law as a degree should really be regarded as a liberal education, rather than a vocational subject.'

'The primary criterion applied in selecting applicants for interview is evidence of general ability. Clear-mindedness, a conceptual approach and a high level of oral facility are also advantageous.'

'Four qualities are highly desirable, exactness, conciseness, strict relevance and system. The best school subjects to take are those which encourage these qualities; the worst are those which ensure success not by the exercise of the grey matter, but by wordy expositions of memorised facts of a merely descriptive nature. A widespread notion which has to be scotched is that science is a worse preparation than arts subjects for law.'

The following is taken from the Bristol University prospectus.

What Qualities of Mind do you Need?

The academic study of law involves the acquisition of the basic knowledge of a subject, the understanding of it, the ability to apply such knowledge relevantly and accurately, and a willingness to criticise the existing law intelligently. Students must be prepared to think for themselves and to develop their own ideas.

It follows that successful law students will have the ability to:

a) understand and assimilate many concepts, principles, rules and large amounts of detailed information;
b) apply their knowledge in a logical, accurate, intelligent manner;
c) analyse subtle legal distinctions; and
d) develop their critical faculties so that they can approach the study of law from a reforming, constructive viewpoint. The student who has assimilated the necessary materials and has learnt to think accurately about legal concepts will have the necessary tools to speculate on what the law ought to be – an important part of legal study.

A Popular Misconception

Despite all the attention given to Criminal Law in the newspapers and on television, a brief glance at the Bristol prospectus will reveal how misconceived it would be to equate the study of Law with an analysis of the Criminal Law. In fact, in the Bristol Law Faculty, Criminal Law is only one of the 14 courses which students undertake for the LLB degree. This is not to say that the study of Criminal Law is unimportant: rather, it is to emphasise that any law course involves a study of various categories of law. One important area of law relates to the obligations that citizens owe each other (studied, for example, in Tort and Contract); another body of law is concerned with rights over property (for example, Land Law); a third is the relationship between the citizen and state institutions (for example, Administrative Law). Students may expect to undertake courses in each of these areas.

The following books should prove useful to anyone who wishes to obtain a general idea of what the study of law may involve:

P Kenny, *Studying Law.*
J A G Griffith, *The Politics of the Judiciary*
P S Atiyah, *Law and Modern Society.*
P Harris, *An Introduction to Law.*
P D Fraser, *How to Pass Law Exams* (HLT Publications 1991).

6   LAW COURSES IN THE UK

First degree courses in law all follow a similar pattern and consist of both compulsory and optional subjects. Compulsory subjects cover legal principles, eg Contract, Criminal Law, Constitutional Law, Land Law, Tort and Equity. Optional subjects, however, cover a very wide field and, for example, at Newcastle University include Civil Liberties, Consumer Protection, Environmental Law, European Community Law, Insurance and Partnership, and Public International Law.

The following universities, polytechnics and colleges offer degree courses in Law (NB Scottish institutions offer Scottish Law). It should be noted that for courses in law combined with other subjects only a small number of places are usually available.

In the near future all polytechnics will be permitted to call themselves 'universities', thus many name changes will therefore take place and readers should be prepared to acquaint themselves with the new names as they become official. The polytechnic title, however, will be retained on applications being submitted from September to December 1992.

Aberdeen University
Aberystwyth University
Anglia Polytechnic
Belfast University
Birmingham Polytechnic
Birmingham University
Bournemouth Polytechnic
Bristol Polytechnic
Bristol University
Brunel University
Buckingham University
Cambridge University
Cardiff University
Central London Polytechnic (London)
City Polytechnic (London)
City University
Coventry Polytechnic
Dundee University
Durham University
East Anglia University
East London Polytechnic
Edinburgh University
Essex University
Exeter University
Glasgow University

Hatfield Polytechnic
Holborn College (London)
Huddersfield Polytechnic
Hull University
Keele University
Kent University
Kingston Polytechnic
Lancashire Polytechnic
Lancaster University
Leeds Polytechnic
Leeds University
Leicester Polytechnic
Leicester University
Liverpool Polytechnic
Liverpool University
London University (King's College)
London (London School of Economics)
London (Queen Mary Westfield College)
London (School of Oriental and African
    Studies)
London (University College)
Luton College of Higher Education
Manchester Polytechnic
Manchester University
Middlesex Polytechnic

Nene College, Northampton	South West Polytechnic
Newcastle-upon-Tyne Polytechnic	Staffordshire Polytechnic
Newcastle University	Southampton University
North London Polytechnic	Stirling University
Nottingham Polytechnic	Strathclyde University
Nottingham University	Surrey University
Oxford Polytechnic	Sussex University
Oxford University	Teesside Polytechnic
Reading University	Wales Polytechnic
Sheffield City Polytechnic	Warwick University
Sheffield University	West London Polytechnic
South Bank Polytechnic	Wolverhampton Polytechnic

Business Law Courses
Bournemouth (Poly), Brunel (Univ), City (Poly) (Business and Finance Law), Coventry (Poly), Huddersfield (Poly), Stirling (Univ) (Business Law and also Business Law and Economics), Surrey (Univ)

European Law
Buckingham (Univ) (English and European Law with French or German), Essex (Univ), Exeter (Univ), Lancaster (Univ) (European Legal Studies), Sussex (Univ), Warwick (Univ)

English and European Laws/Legal systems
East Anglia (Univ), Essex (Univ), London (QMW), Reading (Univ)

English and French Law
Aberdeen (Univ), Buckingham (Univ), Essex (Univ), Kent (Univ), London (King's), London (LSE), London (UC), Manchester (Univ), Reading (Univ), West London (Poly)

English and German Law
Aberdeen (Univ), Buckingham (Univ), East Anglia (Univ), Kent (Univ), London (King's), London (LSE), London (UC), West London (Poly)

English and Spanish Law
Kent (Univ)

European Legal Systems
Lancaster (Univ)

Law with French
Aberdeen (Univ), Buckingham (Univ), Kent (Univ) (Law with a Language), Manchester (Poly), Sussex (Univ) (European Studies), West London (Poly)

Law with German
Aberdeen (Univ), Buckingham (Univ), Kent (Univ) (Law with a Language), Sussex (European Studies), West London (Poly)

Law with Government
Manchester (Poly)

Law with Italian Law
London (UC)

Law with European Studies
Bristol (Poly) (European Law and languages – subject to approval), Exeter (Univ), Sussex (Univ) (European Studies)

Subject Combinations with Law
(Check with universities to establish what exemptions from Law Society examinations are possible with these combinations)

Accountancy
Aberystwyth (Univ), Belfast (Univ), City (Poly), Derbyshire (CHE), Edinburgh (Univ), Kent (Univ), Lancashire (Poly), Leicester (Poly), Manchester (Univ), Newcastle (Univ), Oxford (Poly), Sheffield City (Poly), Southampton (Univ)

African Language
London (SOAS)

American Studies
Derbyshire (CHE), Keele (Univ), Lancashire (Poly), Middlesex (Poly), Nene (College), Wolverhampton (Poly)

Amharic
London (SOAS)

Anthropology
London (LSE), Oxford (Poly)

Applied Education
Oxford (Poly)

Applied Physics
Hatfield (Poly), Lancashire (Poly)

Applied Science
Middlesex (Poly)

Applied Statistics
Oxford (Poly)

Arabic
London (SOAS)

Art and Design
City (Poly), East London (Poly), Nene (College), Sheffield City (Poly)

Art History
East London (Poly), Middlesex (Poly)

Art for Society
Wolverhampton (Poly)

Asian Language
London (SOAS)

Astronomy
Hatfield (Poly), Lancashire (Poly)

Audio Visual/Media Studies
Lancashire (Poly)

Bengali
London (SOAS)

Biochemistry
Lancashire (Poly), Liverpool (Poly), Wolverhampton (Poly)

Biological Science
Wolverhampton (Poly)

Biology
Buckingham (Univ), City (Poly), Derbyshire (CHE), East London (Poly), Hatfield (Poly), Leicester (Poly), Nene (College), Oxford (Poly), South West (Poly), Wolverhampton (Poly)

Biomedical Sciences
Liverpool (Poly), Sheffield City (Poly)

Building
Sheffield City (Poly)

Burmese
London (SOAS)

Business
Birmingham (Univ), City (Poly), Derbyshire (CHE), East London (Poly), (Law with Business and also with Business Systems) Edinburgh (Univ), Hatfield (Poly), Lancashire (Poly), Liverpool (Poly), Nene (College), Sheffield City (Poly), Oxford (Poly), Wolverhampton (Poly)

Business French
Lancashire (Poly)

Cartography
Oxford (Poly)

Catering Management
Oxford (Poly), Sheffield City (Poly)

Celtic
Edinburgh (Univ)

Ceramics
Wolverhampton (Poly)

Chemistry
Derbyshire (CHE), Exeter (Univ), Hatfield (Poly), Keele (Univ), Leicester (Poly), Liverpool (Poly), Oxford (Poly), Sheffield City (Poly), Wolverhampton (Poly)

Chinese
Leeds (Univ)

Civil Engineering
Derbyshire (CHE), London (QMW), Sheffield City (Poly)

Classical Studies
Keele (Univ)

Communication Design
Lancashire (Poly)

Communications Studies
City (Poly), Middlesex (Poly), Sheffield City (Poly)

Community Studies
Liverpool (Poly)

Computational Chemistry
Keele (Univ)

Computer-Aided Engineering
Sheffield City (Poly), Wolverhampton (Poly) (Computer Aided Design)

Computer Studies
City (Poly), Derbyshire (CHE), Hatfield (Poly), Keele (Univ), Leicester (Poly), Nene (College), Oxford (Poly), Sheffield City (Poly), South West (Poly), Strathclyde (Univ), Wolverhampton (Poly)

Construction
Sheffield City (Poly)

Countryside Management
Liverpool (Poly)

Criminal Justice
Liverpool (Poly)

Consumer Studies
Liverpool (Poly)

Cypriot Studies
Middlesex (Poly)

Dance
Liverpool (Poly), Middlesex (Poly)

26

Design
City (Poly), Lancashire (Poly) (Design History)

Design Engineering
Lancashire (Poly)

Development Studies
Lancashire (Poly)

Drama
Derbyshire (CHE), Liverpool (Poly), Middlesex (Poly), Nene (College)

Earth Science
Liverpool (Poly), Middlesex (Poly), Nene (College)

Ecology
Liverpool (Poly)

Economics
Aberdeen (Univ), Aberystwyth (Univ), Anglia (Poly), City (Poly), Derbyshire (CHE), Durham (Univ), East London (Poly), Edinburgh (Univ) (also Economic History), Hatfield (Poly), Keele (Univ), Kent (Univ), Lancashire (Poly), Leicester (Univ), Liverpool (Poly), London (QMW), London (SOAS), Middlesex (Poly), Nene (College), Newcastle (Univ), Oxford (Poly), South West (Poly), Sussex (Univ) (Social Sciences), Wolverhampton (Poly)

Economic and Social History
Kent (Univ)

Education
East London (Poly), Middlesex (Poly), Oxford (Poly) Sheffield City (Poly), Wolverhampton (Poly)

Electrical Engineering
Sheffield City (Poly)

Electrical Media
Wolverhampton (Poly)

Electronics
Hatfield (Poly), Keele (Univ), Lancashire (Poly), Leicester (Poly), Wolverhampton (Poly)

Engineering Science
London (QMW), Wolverhampton (Poly)

English
Anglia (Poly), Derbyshire (CHE) (also English for International Business), Keele (Univ), Lancashire (Poly), Middlesex (Poly), Nene (College), Oxford (Poly), Sheffield City (Poly), Wolverhampton (Poly)

Environmental Studies
City (Poly), Derbyshire (CHE), East London (Poly), Hatfield (Poly), Lancashire (Poly) (Environmental Management), Middlesex (Poly), Nene (College), Oxford (Poly), Wolverhampton (Poly)

Estate Management
Sheffield City (Poly)

European Business
Sheffield City (Poly)

European Language
Aberystwyth (Univ)

European Law and Languages
Bristol (Poly)

European Studies
East London (Poly), Wolverhampton (Poly)

European Thought
Anglia (Poly)

Fashion
Lancashire (Poly)

Film and TV Studies
Derbyshire (CHE)

Financial Services
City (Poly), Liverpool (Poly)

Fine Art
Wolverhampton (Poly)

Food Marketing
Sheffield City (Poly)

Food Science and Nutrition
Oxford (Poly)

French
Aberdeen (Univ), Anglia (Poly), Belfast (Univ), Birmingham (Univ), Bristol (Univ), Cardiff (Univ), City (Poly), Derbyshire (CHE), East London (Poly), Edinburgh (Univ), Keele (Univ), Leicester (Univ), Liverpool (Univ), Liverpool (Poly), Manchester (Poly), Middlesex (Poly), Oxford (Poly), South West (Poly), Surrey (Univ), Wolverhamptom (Poly)

French/German
Keele (Univ)

Geography
Anglia (Poly), City (Poly), Derbyshire (CHE), Lancashire (Poly), Liverpool (Poly), Middlesex (Poly), Nene (College), Oxford (Poly), South West (Poly), Wolverhampton (Poly)

Geology
City (Poly), Derbyshire (CHE), Oxford (Poly)

German
Aberdeen (Univ), Anglia (Poly), Bristol (Univ), Cardiff (Univ), City (Poly), Derbyshire (CHE), East Anglia (Univ), East London (Poly), Edinburgh (Univ), Keele (Univ), Lancashire (Poly) (inc Business German), Liverpool (Univ), Liverpool (Poly), Middlesex (Poly), Oxford (Poly), South West (Poly), Surrey (Univ), Wolverhampton (Poly)

Glass Designs
Wolverhampton (Poly)

Government
Kent (Univ), Manchester (Poly)

Graphic Design
Wolverhampton (Poly)

Gujarati
London (SOAS)

Hausa
London (SOAS)

Hindi
London (SOAS)

Health
Lancashire (Poly), East London (Poly), Lancashire (Poly), Liverpool (Poly), Wolverhampton (Poly)

Health Care
Sheffield City (Poly)

History
Anglia (Poly), City (Poly), Derbyshire (CHE) (inc Studies in Art/Photography), East Anglia (Univ) (English History), Keele (Univ) (also International History), Kent (Univ), Lancashire (Poly), Liverpool (Poly), London (SOAS), Middlesex (Poly), Nene (College), Oxford (Poly), Wolverhampton (Poly), Sheffield City (Poly), Sussex (Univ)

History of Art
Lancashire (Poly), Oxford (Poly), Sheffield City (Poly), Wolverhampton (Poly)

History of Design
Lancashire (Poly)

History of Ideas
Middlesex (Poly)

Home Economics
Liverpool (Poly)

Horticulture
Lancashire (Poly)

Hotel Management
Sheffield City (Poly)

Housing
Sheffield City (Poly)

Human Resource Management
Keele (Univ), Liverpool (Poly)

Illustration
Wolverhampton (Poly)

Indonesian Studies
London (SOAS)

Industrial Relations
Kent (Univ)

Information and Library Studies
Aberystwyth (Univ)

Information Technology
City (Poly), Derbyshire (CHE), East London (Poly), Liverpool (Poly) (Information Management), Middlesex (Poly), Sheffield City (Poly), Wolverhampton (Poly)

International Politics
Keele (Univ)

International Relations and Jurisprudence
Aberdeen (Univ)

Italian
Anglia (Poly), Cardiff (Univ), South West (Poly)

Japanese
Cardiff (Univ), Leeds (Univ), Liverpool (Poly)

Latin
Keele (Univ)

Law and Social Policy
Liverpool (Poly)

Librarianship
Aberystwyth (Univ)

Literature, Life and Thought
East London (Poly), Liverpool (Poly)

Linguistics
Wolverhampton (Poly)

Logistics and Purchasing
Derbyshire (CHE)

Manufacturing Engineering
Lancashire (Poly), Sheffield City (Poly), Wolverhampton (Poly)

Management Studies
Keele (Univ), Lancashire (Poly)

Marathi
London (SOAS)

Marketing
City (Poly), Derbyshire (CHE), Leicester (Poly), Liverpool (Poly)

Materials Engineering
Sheffield City (Poly), Wolverhampton (Poly)

Mathematics
Anglia (Poly), City (Poly), Derbyshire (CHE), East London (Poly), Keele (Univ), Lancashire (Poly), Leicester (Poly), Nene (College), Oxford (Poly), Wolverhampton (Poly), Sheffield City (Poly)

Mechanical Engineering
London (QMW), Sheffield City (Poly)

Media Design
East London (Poly), Liverpool (Poly), Wolverhampton (Poly)

Media Studies
Middlesex (Poly), Wolverhampton (Poly)

Microbiology
Liverpool (Poly)

Microelectronic Systems
Derbyshire (CHE), Oxford (Poly)

Minerals Estate Management
Sheffield City (Poly)

Modern Hebrew
London (SOAS)

Music
Anglia (Poly), Derbyshire (CHE), Keele (Univ) (Electronic Music), Middlesex (Poly), Nene (College), Oxford (Poly), Wolverhampton (Poly)

Natural Science
Middlesex (Poly)

New Technology
East London (Poly)

Operational Research
Hatfield (Poly)

Organisation Studies
Lancashire (Poly)

Painting
Wolverhampton (Poly)

Philosophy
Edinburgh (Univ), Hatfield (Poly), Hull (Univ), Keele (Univ), Kent (Univ), Middlesex (Poly), Wolverhampton (Poly)

Philosophy and Jurisprudence
Aberdeen (Univ)

Photography
Derbyshire (CHE), Wolverhampton (Poly)

Physical Geography
Middlesex (Poly)

Physical Sciences
Oxford (Poly)

Physics
Derbyshire (CHE), Hatfield (Poly), Leicester (Poly), Liverpool (Poly), Oxford (Poly), Sheffield City (Poly), Wolverhampton (Poly)

Physiology/Pharmacology
Lancashire (Poly)

Planning Studies
Liverpool (Poly), Oxford (Poly)

Politics
Aberystwyth (Univ), Birmingham (Univ), Buckingham (Univ), Cardiff (Univ), City (Poly), Durham (Univ), Edinburgh (Univ), Hull (Univ), Keele (Univ), Lancashire (Poly), Liverpool (Poly), London (QMW), London (SOAS), Middlesex (Poly), Nottingham (Univ), Oxford (Poly), South West (Poly), Southampton (Univ), Wolverhampton (Poly)

Politics and Jurisprudence
Aberdeen (Univ)

Popular Culture
East London (Poly)

Printmaking
Derbyshire (CHE), Wolverhampton (Poly)

Psychology
City (Poly), East London (Poly), Keele (Univ), Lancashire (Poly), Liverpool (Poly), Middlesex (Poly), Nene (College), Oxford (Poly), Sheffield City (Poly), South West (Poly), Wolverhampton (Poly)

Psycho-social Studies
East London (Poly)

Public Administration
Sheffield City (Poly)

Public Relations
Lancashire (Poly)

Publishing
Middlesex (Poly), Oxford (Poly)

Quantitative Studies
Middlesex (Poly)

Racism and Ethnicity
Wolverhampton (Poly)

Recreation Management
Sheffield City (Poly)

Religious Studies
Derbyshire (CHE), London (SOAS), Middlesex (Poly), Wolverhampton (Poly)

Retail Management
Oxford (Poly)

Russian
Liverpool (Poly), Middlesex (Poly), Surrey (Univ), Wolverhampton (Poly)

Science, Technology and Sociology
Middlesex (Poly), South West (Poly) (Science), Wolverhampton (Poly)

Sculpture
Wolverhampton (Poly)

Social Anthropology
Kent (Univ), London (SOAS)

Social Policy
East London (Poly), Edinburgh (Univ), Lancashire (Poly), Middlesex (Poly), Sheffield City (Poly), Wolverhampton (Poly)

Social Sciences
Derbyshire (CHE)

Social Studies
Liverpool (Poly), Sheffield City (Poly)

Society
Exeter (Univ)

Sociology
Anglia (Poly), Cardiff (Univ), City (Poly), Durham (Univ), East London (Poly), Edinburgh (Univ), Hull (Univ), Keele (Univ), Kent (Univ), Lancashire (Poly), Liverpool (Poly), Middlesex (Poly), Nene (College), Oxford (Poly), South West (Poly), Warwick (Univ), Wolverhampton (Poly)

Sociology and Jurisprudence
Aberdeen (Univ)

Software Engineering
Derbyshire (CHE)

South East Asian Studies
Kent (Univ)

Soviet and East European Studies
Wolverhampton (Poly)

Spanish
Anglia (Poly), City (Poly), East London (Poly), Lancashire (Poly) (Business Spanish), Middlesex (Poly), South West (Poly), Wolverhampton (Poly)

Sports Studies
Wolverhampton (Poly)

Statistics
City (Poly), Hatfield (Poly), Kent (Univ) (Social Statistics), Lancashire (Poly), Sheffield City (Poly), South West (Poly)

Swahili
London (SOAS)

Tamil
London (SOAS)

Technology
Lancashire (Poly), South West (Poly)

Text and Image
Anglia (Poly)

Thai Studies
London (SOAS)

Theatre Studies
Wolverhampton (Poly)

Third World Studies
East London (Poly), Middlesex (Poly)

Three Dimensional Studies
Lancashire (Poly), Wolverhampton (Poly)

Tourism
Derbyshire (CHE), Oxford (Poly), Sheffield City (Poly)

Trade Union Studies
Middlesex (Poly)

Transport
South West (Poly)

Urban Land Economics
Sheffield City (Poly)

Urban Studies
Liverpool (Poly), Middlesex (Poly), Sheffield City (Poly), Wolverhampton (Poly)

Urdu
London (SOAS)

Vietnamese Studies
London (SOAS)

Visual Arts
Middlesex (Poly)

Visual Communications
Derbyshire (CHE), Wolverhampton (Poly)

Visual Studies
Derbyshire (CHE), Lancashire (Poly), Oxford (Poly)

War Studies
Wolverhampton (Poly)

West European Studies
Wolverhampton (Poly)

Women's Studies
East London (Poly), Lancashire (Poly), Liverpool (Poly), Middlesex (Poly), Wolverhampton (Poly)

Writing
Derbyshire (CHE), Middlesex (Poly)

Other Courses

Courses in Criminology combined with American Studies, Classical Studies, Computer Studies, Economics, French, History, Music, Philosophy, Psychology and Sociology are offered at Keele University.

A course in Criminal Justice is available at Liverpool Polytechnic as a single honours course or in combination with Economics, Health Studies, History, Politics or Sociology.

Courses in Jurisprudence are combined with Sociology, Politics, Philisophy and International Relations at Aberdeen University. Business Law is offered with Economics at Stirling University.

7 THE UNIVERSITY OF LONDON LAW DEGREE STUDIED EXTERNALLY: LLB (London)

In section 5 reference was made to external degree courses, and since the nature and structure of these degrees is largely misunderstood they are worthy of closer consideration.

London University degrees are highly regarded degrees throughout the world and students may choose to study for this degree as external students or as internal students. Internal students study at a College within the University whilst external students choose to study at an independent college such as Holborn College (one of the largest law schools in the UK) or entirely by private study using subject guides and reading lists provided by the University.

Lord Flowers (ex-Vice Chancellor of London University) describes these degrees in greater detail. 'The University does not have separate internal and external degrees. It has a single degree which is studied by internal and external students. The University has always refused to separate the awards available to external students from those for internal students. The reason for this policy is to ensure that the standard of achievement of internal and external students is judged on exactly the same basis. Thus the method of study is not an issue; the important test is the examination. In many instances internal and external students sit exactly the same examination papers for their degree. Where this is not the case the same examiners will have set the papers for external as for internal students. All examination papers, whether for internal or external students are marked by University of London academic staff to exactly the same standard, and the same degree classification is used for both kinds of student.'

Both internal and external students must register as students of the University of London. All students attend the University of London graduation ceremony on graduation where the degrees are presented by the Chancellor, HRH The Princess Royal. No distinction is made between external and internal students when the degree is awarded.

External degrees generally were first introduced by the University of London in the nineteenth century and were created for students unable to attend a London University College either because they could not attend a full time course of study for financial or other reasons or because they did not have the necessary entry requirements for London University Colleges.

It is a well accepted fact that 'A' Level results are not necessarily indicators of degree performance. Students can obtain poor 'A' Level grades for a variety of reasons – they may choose the wrong subjects, they may have poor teachers, or they may experience personal problems during their period of study. This does not mean that they are incapable of degree level study. Regrettably, because the educational system in the UK decides a student's fate on the strength of 'A' Level results many able students are denied the opportunity of proving that they are capable of taking a degree and that their disappointing 'A' Level grades are not a true reflection of their ability. This is overcome by the lower level of offers made by Holborn College for all applicants. The offers set by the London University for External degree students are two passes at Grade E. It should be noted that mature students (over 21) are also always offered places for law courses at universities and polytechnics, with much lower offers than those made to school leavers (in many cases EE offers).

Despite this, a high success rate in the final examinations is achieved each year, largely due to the unique and highly structured teaching system offered by the College. In addition several students obtain university convocation prizes.

Courses are offered for the full three year honours degree programme on a full-time, part-time, re-sit, revision or correspondence course basis.

London University LLB degrees are recognised by the Council of Legal Education and the Law Society for entry to the vocational stage of training. Many Bar Associations world-wide also recognise the degree for entry to their Bar examinations.

Applications to Holborn College are made direct, so if you are aiming for these degrees then it would be wise to submit an application early. (Details can be obtained from: The Registrar, HLT (Holborn College) Group of Colleges, 200 Greyhound Road, London W14 9RY. Tel 071 385 3377.)

Entrance Requirements for Law Degree Students

It is a well accepted fact that 'A' Level results are not necessarily indicators of potential performance on degree courses. Students can obtain poor 'A' Level grades for a variety of reasons – perhaps they have chosen the wrong subjects, they may have had poor teaching, or they may have experienced personal problems during their period of study. Poor performance on the day of the 'A' Level examination does not mean that a student is incapable of degree level study. Regrettably, because the educational system in the United Kingdom decides a student's educational fate largely on the strength of 'A' level results, many able students are denied the opportunity of proving that they are capable of taking a degree and that their disappointing 'A' Level grades are not a true reflection of their ability.

Because there is intense competition for places on law degree courses at universities, polytechnics and colleges of higher education in the United Kingdom, the 'A' Level grades required for admission tend to be fairly high. The University of London's external degree in Law (see Chapter 5) accepts students for registration for the degree examinations if they meet its 'general entrance requirements' comprising a total of five GCSE/GCE passes of which two must be at Advanced Level (Grade E or above), two 'AS' level passes at Grade C or above are accepted as one 'A' level pass. Most of the colleges offering courses leading to the University of London's external LLB degree accept students who meet the University's registration requirement and do not stipulate higher 'A' Level grades for entry.

It should be noted that, in most cases, students over the age of 21 years are considered as 'mature students' and whether they are applying for 'internal' or 'external' degree courses, concessions are often made if they do not possess the high 'A' Level grades required of school or college leavers for direct entry to degree courses.

Admissions Officers will normally consider applications from 'mature' students with low 'A' level grades or indeed without 'A' Levels where the applicants can show evidence of some academic study (since leaving full-time education), motivation and even relevant work and in-service training experience. Facilities exist for students to follow part-time or distance learning courses while continuing in their full-time employment. Many course programmes (such as the University of London's external LLB and the LLB (Honours) Degree by Distance Learning, an external degree offered by Holborn College in association with Wolverhampton Polytechnic) allow flexibility in styles of study and enable students to change from distance learning study to full-time or part-time study at any stage of the course programme.

Holborn College in London has been preparing students for the University of London's external LLB degree examinations for more than twenty years, and largely due to its unique and highly structured teaching system, its students achieve high success rates each year with several obtaining University Convocation Prizes. The College, which is an Associate College of Wolverhampton Polytechnic, also offers a full-time internal LLB (Honours) degree course which provides the same well-proven teaching system geared to a course programme devised, taught and examined jointly by staff of Wolverhampton Polytechnic and Holborn College – an example of co-operation between the public and independent sectors of higher education in the United Kingdom.

Applications for courses at Holborn College are made direct, so students aiming for the University of London external LLB degree courses or for the Holborn College/Wolverhampton Polytechnic LLB full-time or distance learning degrees should submit an early application to: The Registrar, Holborn College, 200 Greyhound Road, London W14 9RY (Tel 071 385 3377). Details of the Univeristy of London's external LLB degree can be obtained from The Secretary for External Students, Room 201, Senate House, University of London, Malet Street, London WC1E 7HU. (Tel 071 636 8000).

8 APPLYING FOR DEGREE COURSES

It is often assumed that all applicants automatically apply only for university places. This is not so. Everyone is different, not only in their attitudes towards higher education but also in the subjects they wish to study, where they wish to study and what their ultimate career targets may be.

You must therefore consider all aspects of your application including your objectives and in particular your abilities.

Your success or failure in obtaining a place will be largely determined by your exam results and also by your projected grades at 'A' Level as shown on your referees' report.

This is why a careful strategy is needed. *Never assume you will get the place you want at the institution you want.* YOU MUST CONSIDER ALL THE ALTERNATIVES.

How can you do this?

a) Choose your course and check the prospectuses of each university, polytechnic and college offering the course.

b) Having decided which institutions offer interesting courses then refer to *The Complete Degree Course Offers* (HEAPS Bookshop, £11.95, postage £1.00). This is the only reference book which lists the courses offered in all universities, polytechnics and colleges and provides information on the selection policies adopted, including the level of offers made to applicants, interview questions and many other aspects which concern your chances of an acceptance.

Obtain advice from your 'A' Level subject tutors concerning the grades you could achieve in the examinations. In this way you can judge your chances of being considered by the university, polytechnic or college of your initial choice. If your chances don't look too hopeful, consider those other institutions which might seriously consider you.

Universities are generally more popular than other institutions and because of this their offers are usually the highest. The basis of any application strategy however is to cover yourself in case your 'A' Level grades don't match the offers made by your universities. All universities set their grades against the number of applications and the number of places available; thus the more popular the institution the higher the offer.

In short, universities are more popular than polytechnics and polytechnics are more popular than Colleges and Institutes of Higher Education. The most popular institutions, however, must never be regarded necessarily as the 'best'. In the case of law courses, most institutions are offering the same type of course and only the optional subjects are likely to differ between one institution and the next. The most popular institutions are usually those located in popular geographical areas such as

Oxford, Cambridge, Bristol, Durham, Exeter, Warwick and Nottingham which attracts many students because of its campus. Similarly, polytechnics in Oxford and Bristol are also very popular – again because of their location.

YOUR STRATEGY must be to make sure that you include on your application forms some institutions which may make you lower offers. In this way you will cover yourself against a poor exam result.

In addition to exam results, however, some admissions tutors place quite a lot of importance on interviews. Interviews come in all 'shapes and sizes'. Sometimes it will be a straightforward 'one to one' interview. In other cases you may face two, three or even (rarely) four interviewers.

In the case of law interviews, however, admissions tutors will expect you to be 'well read': to be familiar with current legal issues and in prominent law cases which have aroused much public discussion.

(*The Complete Degree Course Offers* also lists the questions which have been asked in past years and whilst interviews will vary from year to year you will be able to judge what admissions tutors expect you to know.)

In Section 12 universities, polytechnics and colleges are listed, their sizes and their locations, and all those important considerations which must be made when deciding where to study.

Application

The next stage is equally important – submitting your applications – and for those aiming for careers in law there are three main alternatives.

a)   for universities (and some colleges) applications are submitted through the UCCA scheme; and

b)   for polytechnics (and some colleges) the PCAS scheme.

(There is one application form for both these schemes).

c)   for other colleges, which are not in either of these schemes (eg Holborn College), applications are made direct to the college concerned.

The mode of application is shown against the names of institutions in Chapter 12.

Once you have decided on the course of study you wish to follow (and if you are applying to universities) you *must check* the subjects required by the university and also by the Faculty or Department of the university.

There are two types of entry requirements: general requirements and course requirements.

General Requirements

Each institution stipulates certain GCSE (or equivalent) subject requirements *for all their courses,* irrespective of whether or not these are arts, science or social science courses. ('AS' Level, 'AO' Level or 'A' Level passes are also acceptable instead of GCSE Grades A–C or 'O' Level passes.)

(Check with university and polytechnic prospectuses that you have the right general requirements for your chosen course at the institution to which you intend to apply).

'A' Levels, 'AS' Levels, GCSE (or equivalent)
Minimum entry requirements by way of the numbers of 'A' Levels, 'AS' Levels and GCSE subjects are also stipulated by each university. In the majority of cases most students will automatically qualify because of the subjects being taken in these examinations. It is, however, wise to check these requirements, particularly if you only achieved Grade A–C passes in a small number of subjects at GCSE or equivalent. For example, the minimum entry requirement at all universities is that of two 'A' Level passes and three Grade A–C passes in the GCSE exams. THESE PASSES MUST BE IN DIFFERENT SUBJECTS.

Course Requirements

Many different subjects are offered at 'A' Level – including several subjects of a vocational nature such as Accountancy, Art, Business Studies, Theatre Studies, Communication Studies and Psychology, Music, Home Economics, Engineering Drawing and Technology.

Many university courses have a very strong academic (non vocational) bias, the purpose of the course being to provide you with a broad 'education' and not a 'training' for a specific job, and consequently universities often tend to prefer the purely academic subjects such as English, Geography, History, Religious Studies, Languages and Science subjects. For certain courses, therefore, they may not accept the more vocational 'A' Level subjects. CHECK THE LIST OF APPROVED SUBJECTS IN THE PROSPECTUS.

It must also be noted that some 'A' Level subjects are similar in subject matter, such as Art and the History of Art, and Law and Constitutional Law, and these subjects may only be counted as one 'A' Level, even though you may have chosen them as two separate subjects, for exam purposes.

Now let us take a look at the application schemes in more detail.

The UCCA/PCAS form

As in the case with all application forms, you should read through the form carefully beforehand to familiarise yourself with all the information you are asked to provide. UCCA (Universities Central Council on Admissions) and PCAS (Polytechnics Central Admission System), however, also publish their respective handbooks and you MUST also read through these instructions prior to completing the form.

It is also very important to remember that when your form is received by UCCA or PCAS, a photocopy is made of it which is reduced in size *almost by half*. Neat handwriting or printing is therefore essential. Typing is acceptable.

The main sections on the current (1991) form are as follows (some minor changes may appear on the 1992 forms).

1   *Surname/Family name, Correspondence address/postcode/telephone, Home address/postcode/telephone*
     Depending on your personal circumstances you should remember that you could receive instructions or advice from your universities, polytechnics or colleges during Christmas, Easter and Summer vacations. Students at boarding schools, for example, should use an address (probably their home address) from which such information can be forwarded without delay.

2   *Personal details*
     Some of this information needs to be coded. Details of these codes are provided in the UCCA/PCAS handbook.

3A   *Universities/Colleges in the UCCA Scheme*

3B   *Polytechnics/Colleges in the PCAS Scheme*
     All courses in the UCCA and PCAS Schemes are listed in the respective handbooks. When you have decided on your subject you will need to give details by way of the university, polytechnic or college code name, the university, polytechnic or college code number, the course code and the course code name. All these details are given in the UCCA/PCAS handbooks.
     In many cases you will wish to apply for the same subject at each of your universities, polytechnics or colleges. However, problems may occur if you wish to (or have to) mix your subject choices. For example there are some non-law subjects in which only one or two courses are offered, such as Retail Management, Brewing, Animal Nutrition and Wildlife Management. In such cases it may be necessary to consider other subjects to go on your application form and you should choose subjects which are similar in subject content, eg Business Studies courses with Retail Management, Chemistry with Brewing, Animal Sciences with Animal Nutrition, or Ecology with Wildlife Management. However, if you are choosing very popular subjects such as Medicine, Veterinary Science, Pharmacy or Law then you should not mix these with any other subjects in Sections 3a or 3b. Admissions tutors are looking for motivation and any evidence that interests are divided may result in a rejection.
     It is, however, possible to vary your course choices if they have a common element running through them such as combined courses with history, as below:

     History/Spanish
     History/Philosophy
     History/Religious Studies
     History/Spanish
     History/Spanish

     On the UCCA section of the form you are permitted to apply for up to five courses. On the PCAS section of the form you may apply for up to four courses. All institutions to which you apply are listed alphabetically and there is no way in which you can show a preference for any institution.
     Most candidates wish to submit the maximum number of course choices in each of the sections 3a and/or 3b although there is no reason why you should

43

not limit your applications to one, two or three if you so wish. Similarly it is also quite in order to apply for two different courses at the same university (except at Oxford or Cambridge) providing there are similarities in the courses chosen). Some candidates do this because they wish to increase their chances of getting a place at a certain university.

4   *Planning statistics (occupational background and ethnic origin)*
     This information is of interest to universities, polytechnics and colleges, but does not affect your chances of being rejected.

5A   *Academic qualifications (examinations for which the results are known)*
     All examinations taken, including the failures, must be listed.

5B   *Academic qualifications (examinations to be taken or results pending)*

5C   *Academic qualifications (BTEC, SCOTVEC)*

6   *Education from age 11 in date order*

7   *Details of employment to date*

8   *Name and address of sponsor*

9   *Further information*
     This is a very important section and one which requires careful preparation. It is the only section on the form in which you can 'speak for yourself'. It is in this section that your character and interests can emerge and if you are applying for a vocational course such as Medicine or Law then you should be able to provide information about your interests in these fields, such as hospital employment or visits to the law courts etc.

     For vocational courses, motivation is extremely important and inevitably applicants will wish to impress the admissions tutor. This, however, should not be done by stating how clever, imaginative, hard-working or deserving you are (it has been known for applicants to write glowing references for themselves in this section!). Your teachers will submit their references concerning your attitude and your ability in the examinations (including their assessment of what grades you will probably achieve at 'A' Level).

     If you are applying for a vocational course, such as business studies, then work experience is extremely important.

A simple statement, for example, that you have worked on the cashout at a supermarket is not enough. Try to describe what you learned whilst doing it! Customer problems and attitudes. How did you deal with difficult customers? Did difficult customers fall into any particular age range? What problems did they cause? How did you get on with your fellow workers? Was there a good spirit among the workforce? What did other assistants feel about the management? Was the store well managed? If not, what were the problems? What problems did the management face? Could these problems be easily overcome or were they dictated by Head Office? Was the store well laid out? Was it necessary to make changes to the store layout to increase sales? Was it a profitable store? If not, why not. What was the customer profile – were the majority of shoppers teenagers, middle age female or old people?

By describing some of these aspects of your work experience in detail you have proved that you are aware of what business is about, that you are alert and, above all, that you have taken a real interest in at least one aspect of business. This also applies to other types of work experience.

Some people find it difficult to fill these sections, but others run out of space very quickly! Firstly, you do not have to write an essay. You can save space by not writing in prose. You need to plan it out carefully beforehand, however, and get your parents to help you – they will probably be able to remember some of the things you have done in the past years which you have forgotten all about! This is indeed the purpose of this section. Admissions tutors want a 'profile' of the type of person you are – your interests and your achievements.

It is usual to go back in time about three years – the fact that you were a milk monitor eight years ago in primary school will probably not carry much weight. However, if you won a national speaking competition or achieved something equally notable at an early age then this might be worth mentioning.

Plan out the section methodically. This could be done in sub-sections as follows.

School activities

Positions of responsibility, eg school prefect, chairperson, treasurer, secretary of any committees, sporting activities (indoor and outdoor sports), team membership with dates (this will show how long you have been involved with the team). Field courses (more than one day) attended as part of your studies. Business games, school visits abroad. Musical activities – school orchestra – instruments played (if you have taken any music exams, include the grades achieved). School drama productions. If you have taken the lead, name the play and give dates.

Out of school activities

Sport, music, drama, scouts, guides, youth hostelling, fell walking (give name, dates and places visited). Exchange visits abroad.

Work experience

Details of part-time holiday work, particularly if it relates to the subject of your chosen course. Work observation in hospitals, law courts, business organisations etc. (This is important if you are applying for vocational courses.) If you are applying for a vocational course it could be useful to use this sub-section as the main heading.

Proposed career (if decided)

Unless you are applying for a vocational course there is no need to mention a possible future career which is after all at least four years away!

Finally, photocopy your form for your own reference. If you are interviewed they will probably ask questions about some of the points you have mentioned so – BE HONEST!

9   PRACTICE IN THE EUROPEAN COMMUNITY

In 1985, the European Commission suggested a major new approach to tackle restrictions imposed on the harmonisation of the legal and other professions which in effect allows those concerned to practise their profession freely within the community. It put forward a draft directive on higher education diplomas, under which the qualifications necessary to pursue a profession in one Member State will be recognised throughout the community. The directive will apply to all professions to which access is in some way restricted by the state and which require at least three years' university level training or equivalent plus any appropriate job-based training. It will therefore apply to lawyers, accountants, engineers and many others.

The Directive was agreed by the Council of Ministers in December 1988 and Member States should have implemented it by 4 January 1991. It will enable a professional from one Member State to become a member of the equivalent profession in another Member State 'without' having to requalify.

It does so by introducing the principle of mutual recognition; in other words a fully qualified professional in one Member State is deemed to be fully qualified in another, subject to two safeguards designed to maintain professional standards.

The first involves the length of education and training which the professional has received in their own country. If it is shorter than that required in the country to which they wish to move, the professional concerned may be required to produce evidence of up to four years' experience as a fully qualified professional in another EC country in addition to their professional education and training. This ensures that any shortfall in the length of training is made good by professional experience, thus bringing the person concerned up to an equivalent level of expertise.

The second safeguard takes effect where there is a substantial difference in the content of education and training in a given profession between two EC states. This applies even where the length of the two professional training courses is the same. There are two main reasons why the content of a course might differ substantially. Firstly, the actual boundaries of a profession may vary between Member States. Secondly, the boundaries of a profession may be the same but there may be individual subjects which are specific to one Member State and which are essential in order to operate as a fully qualified professional in that state.

In the above situations, incoming professionals may be required to undergo a test or period of supervised practice designed to ensure that they have acquired the extra knowledge needed to be a fully effective professional in the field concerned. It comprises either an examination – known as the 'aptitude test' – or a period of assessed supervised practice – known as the 'adaptation period', not exceeding three years, in the country concerned. It is for the incoming professional to choose between the two. The test must not be too difficult and the adaptation period must not be too long.

In some cases an experienced professional who is already familiar with professional requirements in the country to which he or she is applying may choose to take the test. In other cases, a less experienced professional may choose instead to undergo a period of supervised practice with a fully qualified professional from the country concerned in order to adapt to local conditions.

The Directive provides an exception in which the Member State may specify either an aptitude test or an adaptation period for those professions which require a precise knowledge of national law and involve providing advice on national law as a constant and essential aspect of the professional activity.

Once the Directive is in force, all professionals whose qualifications fall within its scope will have a right to have their qualifications recognised in another Member State. To do so, they should first consult the list of 'competent authorities' – bodies responsible for receiving applications to practice in the relevant Member States. Application will be made along with his or her qualifications and the authority will either:

a)   accept the application and grant recognition to the professional concerned, including the right to use the appropriate title or designatory letters;
b)   require the professional to produce evidence of further professional experience;
c)   require the professional to take an aptitude test or undergo a period of supervised practice;
d)   reject the application.

The competent authority's decision must in any case be supported by reasons and the professional will have a right of appeal to a national court or tribunal.

To take advantage of these opportunities, members of the professions will need to be prepared. Languages are an obvious area for attention. English is widely spoken and understood within the community but knowledge of languages in other Member States will be essential for practising there. A knowledge of the relevant language will be a significant part of the professional's overall marketability.

Here are the relevant addresses which may be of use to those interested:

THE LAW SOCIETY'S SOLICITOR'S EUROPEAN GROUP (SEG)
The Honorary Secretary SEG
The Law Society
Chancery Lane
London WC2A 1PL   Tel: 071 242 1222
Membership fee (annually):
          qualified lawyers – £10.00
          trainees and students – £2.00

INTERNATIONAL BAR ASSOCIATION (IBA)
Office of the Executive Director
2 Harewood Place
Hanover Square
London W1R 9HB   Tel: 071 629 1206
Membership fee (annually):
     depending upon age and extent of
     participation ranging from £18 to about
     £140

UNION INTERNATIONALE DES AVOCATS (UIA)
48 Bedford Square
London WC1B 3DS   Tel: 071 686 8010

OR 1 Brick Court
Temple
London EC4Y 9BY   Tel: 071 583 0777
Membership fee (annually):
     individual members – £60
     young lawyers – £30

ASSOCIATION INTERNATIONALE DES JEUNES AVOCATS (AIJA)
3 Kings Bench Walk
Inner Temple
London EC4Y 7DJ   Tel: 071 936 2050
Membership fee (all qualified lawyers may join AIJA):
     under 30 years of age – 2,800 Belgian Francs
     over 30 years of age – 4,000 Belgian Francs

EUROPEAN LAWYERS UNION/UNION DES AVOCATS EUROPEENS (UAE)
16 St Martins Le Grand
London EC1A 4EJ   Tel: 071 606 8855
Subscription:
     80 ECUs
     40 ECUs (for those under three years qualified)

EUROPEAN ASSOCIATION OF LAWYERS/
ASSOCIATION EUROPEENE DES AVOCATS (EAL)
C A Slinsby
10 New Square
Lincolns Inn
London WC2   Tel: N/A
Membership fee:
     N/A

EUROPEAN LAW STUDENTS ASSOCIATION
The International Relations Officer
Trainee Solicitors Group
The Law Society
Ipsley Court
Redditch
Worcestershire B98 OTD

UNITED KINGDOM ASSOCIATION FOR EUROPEAN LAW (UKAEL)
Executive Secretary
Kings College
Strand
London WC2 2LS   Tel: 071 240 0206
Membership fee (annually):
      for individuals – £5
      corporate/organisation membership – £15

INTERNATIONAL LAW ASSOCIATION (British Branch)
Honorary Secretary
Watling House
35 Cannon Street
London EC4M 5SD   Tel: 071 489 8000

BELGIAN BRITISH JURISTS ASSOCIATION
23 Great Castle Street
London W1R 8NQ   Tel: 071 629 8883

BRITISH ITALIAN LAW ASSOCIATION
Secretary
c/o Braby and Walker
8–9 East Harding Street
London EC4A 3DS   Tel: 071 583 8511

BRITISH GERMAN JURISTS ASSOCIATION
Secretary
c/o Pritchard Englefield and Tobin
23 Great Castle Street
London W1N 8NQ   Tel: 071 629 8883

10 QUALIFYING AT THE BAR IN THE USA

Generally the United States' 'legal market' is open to anyone with basic legal qualifications. Because of the jurisdiction in the fifty different states I have chosen the New York and Californian Bars as examples, in order to demonstrate how the system in America works.

The New York Bar

For the New York Bar, eligibility can only be determined by the New York Board of Law Examiners. It is the responsibility of each applicant to confirm their eligibility with the Board of Examiners. The minimum requirement is a 2:2 degree or its equivalent. The candidate must have completed a three year law degree in order to sit for the Bar examinations. The applicant must also be over 21 years of age. In order to open up the market the applicant is not required to be a resident of New York State or even a citizen of the United States.

The student must demonstrate that he has completed the degree in a law school approved in the country in which it is located and he must also satisfy the Board of Examiners that the degree that he has studied was based on the English Common Law.

The New York Bar examinations themselves are divided into several parts. The New York portion of the examination is based on procedural and substantive law. In addition candidates must sit for the multi-state Bar examination paper which involves 200 multiple choice questions prepared by the National Conference of Bar Examiners. This part of the examination can be taken in another jurisdiction as it is common to all of the 50 states. The third part of the examination is important, this is the multi-state professional responsibility examination. No applicant can be admitted to the New York Bar without successfully completing all these examinations. The multi-state professional responsibility examination consists of multiple choice questions in the field of professional responsibility but is administered by the National Conference of Bar examiners. The examinations are held three times a year in March, August and November. The examinations are conducted in Albany, the capital of New York State.

On passing the examination the candidate is certified as a member of the New York Bar.

The Californian Bar

The Californian Bar is open to candidates who have at least a 2:2 law degree. There are two categories of applicants in California. These are called 'general applicants' and 'attorney applicants'.

General Applicants

General Applicants must be at least 18 years of age and of good moral character. They must have graduated from a college or university approved by the American Bar Association or the Department of Education. Applicants are considered from those with a US law degree, those who have passed the Bar examinations of a sister state in the United States and also from candidates who have obtained similar qualifications overseas where the Common Law of England constitutes the basis of jurisdiction.

Attorney Applicants

Attorney applications must be from other sister states who wish to be admitted to the Californian Bar. A lawyer who is licensed to practise in a country other than the United States must sit for the General Bar Examination no matter how long the candidate has practised in his or her native country.

The examination consists for four parts:

a)   The Californian State Bar examination which is an essay test.
b)   The Multi-state Bar examination.
c)   The Californian State Bar examination which unlike the essay test is a performance test involving drafting inter-relational skills, negotiation etc.
d)   The Multi-State Professional Responsibility Examination which involves some accounts and ethics.

On successful completion of the examination the applicant is certified as a member of the Californian Bar.

Those candidates who are attorney applicants only need to sit for the Multi-State Professional Responsibility Examination if the pass mark in the state in which they have taken the examination is lower than the pass mark for California.

11 GRANTS AND GRADUATE EMPLOYMENT

Grants for higher education are available to home students and certain overseas students if he or she has resided in the UK for at least three years (provided that residence has not been for educational purposes). EC students can also apply as 'home' students but other students will pay higher fees and will not be eligible for grants. A grant at present will cover tuition fees and is paid by the local authority. The maintenance grant will vary depending upon your parents' income although your parents are not necessarily obliged to pay their share! For 1991/92 the maximum maintenance grant will be frozen at £2,265 each year (£2,845 in London) and for students studying at home – £1,795. A system of loans is now operating available to all undergraduates under 50. These loans will have to be paid after you graduate as soon as your salary reaches 85 per cent of the national average wage. In 1991/92 it will be possible for you to borrow up to £580 each year (£660 in London) if you are living away from home and £460 if you study at home.

Full details are given in *Students Grants and Loans* available free of charge from DES, Publications Despatch Centre, Honeypot Lane, Canons Park, Stanmore, Middlesex, HA7 1AZ or from the Scottish Office, Education Department, Gyleview House, 3 Redheughs Rigg, South Gyle, Edinburgh EH12 9HH or from DES, Northern Ireland, Rathgael House, Balloo Road, Bangor, Co Down, BT19 2PR.

Graduate employment

There are more misconceptions about graduate employment than any other aspect of higher education. It is generally firmly believed that a degree course must always be a preparation for a certain career eg Law for the legal profession, English for journalism, French for translating and interpreting and teaching courses for teaching. Nothing could be further from the truth! A four year degree course of teacher training for example can certainly lead to a satisfying career in the classroom, but it is also an excellent preparation for any job dealing with people, and as the following tables show, some graduates go into business, administration and social work from a range of degree subjects.

A degree or diploma course therefore should be seen as an extension to your education. In some cases it will prepare you for a specific career, but it will also open many other doors.

The tables which follow refer to the types of work which new graduates (men and women) entered in 1989 under three headings: a) Universities, b) Polytechnics, c) Colleges and Institutes of Higher Education. (These figures are the most recent available and have been provided by the Department of Education and Science.)

a)   From   Universities   Percentages

DEGREE SUBJECT	Science R&D	Engineering R&D	Science/ Engineering Support	Environmental Planning	Computing etc	Legal Information Services
Engineering:						
General	3	43	4	4	14	1
Civil	-	10	1	76	2	-
Electrical	1	73	3	1	11	-
Electronic	4	61	3	1	19	-
Mechanical	2	71	4	1	3	-
Aeronautical	1	61	2	-	5	1
Chemical	2	66	5	-	6	-
Biology	22	1	12	1	3	3
Botany	21	-	10	1	10	1
Zoology	16	-	9	1	4	5
Microbiology	32	-	23	-	2	1
Biochemistry	36	-	11	-	3	1
Chemistry	32	2	6	-	5	2
Physics	22	19	3	-	19	1
Geology	38	4	8	7	9	-
Maths	3	2	1	-	21	1
Computer science	3	5	1	-	79	-
Geography Sc	2	1	-	9	9	2
Geography SSc	-	-	1	6	6	3
Economics		1			7	2
Business studies		-			7	1
Accountancy		-			1	-
Law		-			2	27
Psychology Sc		5			5	3
Psychology SSc		5			5	4
Sociology		-			2	7
Politics		1			2	4
English		-			3	5
French		-			2	6
German		1			2	10
Classics		1			5	5
Misc langs		-			3	6
History		1			2	5
History of art		-			-	13
Archaeology		4			2	41
Philosophy		-			6	4
Education		-			-	-
ALL SUBJECTS	5	10	2	4	8	2
Men	5	15	2	5	10	1
Women	5	2	2	2	4	4

Creative Enter- tainment	Admin/ Management Trainee	Financial Work	Medicine/ Social Welfare	Teaching	Buying/ Marketing	Secretarial/ Clerical	Total =100%
1	6	16	2	-	5	2	389
-	2	6	1	-	1	1	842
1	3	5	-	-	1	-	267
-	3	5	1	-	2	1	962
-	5	6	1	-	5	3	954
1	16	7	-	-	4	3	189
-	8	8	-	-	3	1	491
2	14	15	6	1	14	8	508
1	19	7	7	-	10	14	73
1	14	13	9	2	17	10	187
-	15	11	2	-	10	3	205
1	10	18	4	1	10	4	470
1	12	24	3	1	9	3	947
1	5	18	3	1	4	3	1072
1	7	12	2	-	7	4	350
1	5	58	2	1	3	2	1194
-	2	4	1	-	2	2	993
2	16	25	8	1	16	9	229
2	21	28	7	1	19	6	670
1	10	63	3	1	10	4	1243
1	23	35	3	-	27	2	985
-	2	94	-	-	1	1	564
3	11	33	6	1	7	9	513
3	8	13	38	5	13	7	475
4	9	9	38	4	14	8	243
4	14	7	38	5	16	8	258
6	23	21	13	1	16	13	388
14	18	11	9	4	22	14	817
3	20	22	8	6	21	13	352
6	21	19	7	4	18	13	160
10	14	29	7	2	17	10	185
6	18	25	5	3	24	9	848
5	17	31	10	1	16	10	1174
17	20	6	3	4	17	22	138
3	11	12	9	2	9	8	116
11	15	14	13	1	14	23	124
1	3	1	2	88	2	2	836
3	9	20	21	3	9	5	36441
2	9	21	17	2	7	4	21575
3	10	17	27	6	11	6	14866

b) From Polytechnics

SUBJECT	Science/ Engineering R&D	Science/ Engineering Support	Environ- mental Planning	Computing	Other Research	Creative/ Enter- tainment
Engineering:						
Civil	6	1	86	-	-	-
Electrical	70	7	1	15	-	-
Mechanical	81	4	2	3	-	-
General	66	3	1	7	1	1
Biological science	34	26	-	2	1	2
Chemistry	47	17	-	3	2	2
Physics	61	6	-	10	-	4
Misc science	27	8	5	10	2	1
Comb science	13	11	2	15	4	3
Maths	6	1	-	74	-	-
Computing	5	1	-	86	-	-
Business		1		8	-	-
Accountancy		-		2	-	-
Economics		2		6	1	-
Geography		13		8	4	1
Govt/pub admin		1		3	3	3
Psychology		3		1	7	1
Sociology		1		2	3	1
Other social studies		1		1	2	7
Law		2		-	38	2
English		1		-	10	7
French/German/Spanish		2		-	11	5
Other languages		2		4	2	3
History		3		2	8	6
Arts general		2		2	6	8
Fine art		2		-	4	57
Design		6		-	1	80
Drama		1		-	-	42
Education		-		1	-	-
ALL SUBJECTS	12	3	11	9	3	8

Admin/ Management Trainee	Financial Work	Medicine/ Social Welfare	Teaching	Buying/ Marketing/ Selling	Secretarial/ Clerical	Total =100%
2	2	-	-	1	-	407
2	1	1	-	2	1	663
5	1	-	-	2	1	512
9	2	2	1	7	1	342
5	6	4	-	11	7	427
9	6	1	-	12	2	265
-	4	-	2	11	2	84
13	8	7	1	8	10	260
17	10	6	1	11	9	800
3	9	1	-	4	1	406
1	1	-	1	2	2	750
17	26	6	-	40	2	1316
2	91	-	-	2	2	676
14	48	4	1	20	5	384
23	12	6	2	18	11	260
28	10	12	2	22	16	196
13	6	40	4	15	9	159
19	7	38	5	12	13	552
14	6	39	3	16	12	397
13	19	7	2	10	7	195
16	7	11	2	21	25	123
19	16	7	2	18	21	57
26	12	9	3	27	10	206
21	13	10	-	17	21	63
21	6	15	5	15	21	507
5	-	7	5	8	12	339
2	-	-	1	5	3	1171
11	2	4	9	17	15	113
1	1	1	94	1	1	1436
10	12	9	9	10	5	16616

c) From Colleges and Institutes of Higher Education   Percentages

SUBJECT	Science/ Engineering R&D	Science/ Engineering Support	Environ- mental Planning	Computing	Other Research	Creative/ Enter- tainment
Misc science	19	5	7	2	1	2
Comb science	3	6	3	5	3	3
Business		-		3	1	-
Accountancy		1		1	-	-
Geography		15		6	2	3
Psychology		4		4	10	-
Sociology		2		1	2	1
Other social studies		2		-	7	13
English		2		2	3	13
Other languages		-		4	12	2
History		1		3	14	4
Arts general		2		1	4	9
Fine art		2		1	5	62
Design		6		-	1	78
Drama		1		3	2	42
Education		-		-	-	-
ALL SUBJECTS ex education	3	2	3	2	4	23

Admin/Management Trainee	Financial Work	Medicine/Social Welfare	Teaching	Buying/Marketing/Selling	Secretarial/Clerical	Total =100%
31	4	5	2	10	12	121
25	6	9	5	19	14	300
16	31	5	-	39	3	146
4	89	-	-	1	3	71
30	11	9	-	12	12	66
4	2	41	18	8	8	49
11	6	54	1	12	11	109
22	7	4	2	28	15	54
23	6	5	6	25	15	112
26	4	5	2	33	12	57
22	5	11	4	22	15	74
25	5	13	5	16	19	766
3	1	5	4	5	13	263
3	-	1	2	5	5	591
13	2	4	3	10	20	127
1	-	1	96	1	1	3027
17	7	11	4	14	11	3529

12 LIST OF UNIVERSITIES, POLYTECHNICS AND COLLEGES

In the near future, Polytechnics will be permitted to use the title 'University'. The title 'Polytechnic', however, will be retained in the PCAS Handbook in 1992 and will be required to be used by students submitting UCCA/PCAS forms from September 1992.

Aberdeen (Univ): The university offers a wide range of courses all of which (except medicine) are fully modularised. There are 6,500 full-time first-degree students 70% Scots. The university's main teaching buildings and its student halls and flats are closely grouped in Old Aberdeen, on the northern side of the city, and there are two city-centre locations, each within a mile of the Old Aberdeen site, for medicine and related sciences. University accommodation is available for half the student population, including all first-year students from outside Aberdeen. (*The University of Aberdeen, Regent Walk, Aberdeen AB9 1FX, Scotland. Tel 0224 272090*) UCCA.

Aberystwyth (Univ): See under Wales (Univ).

Anglia (Poly): The Cambridge base is close to the city centre. Wide range of courses at degree and HND levels. (*Anglia Polytechnic, Cambridge Campus: East Road, Cambridge CB1 1PT. Tel 0223 63271; or Chelmsford Campus:* (and also a site at Brentwood) *Victoria Road South, Chelmsford, Essex CM1 1LL. Tel 0245 493131*) PCAS.

Architectural Association (School of Architecture) Situated in Georgian houses in the centre of London with an international reputation. (*Architectural Association School, 34 Bedford Square, London WC1B 3AS. Tel 071 636 0974*) DIRECT.

Aston (Univ): Forty-acre green city-centre campus in Birmingham. Many new buildings and excellent computing facilities. Three faculties (engineering, science, management and modern languages). 3,600 students, with accommodation for 65% (half on campus). Excellent sports facilities. Two-thirds of students are on sandwich degree programmes. (*Aston University, Aston Triangle, Birmingham B4 7ET. Tel 021 359 6313*) UCCA.

Bangor Normal (Coll): Situated in a residential area of Bangor. 400 students. (*Bangor Normal College, Bangor, Gwynedd, North Wales LL57 2PX. Tel 0248 370171*) PCAS.

Bangor (Univ): See under Wales (Univ).

Bath (CHE): Two sites about 2 miles outside Bath. 1,300 students. (*Bath College of Higher Education, Newton Park, Bath BA2 9BN. Tel 0225 873701*) PCAS.

60

Bath (Univ): This popular university was founded in 1966 on a campus site overlooking the city. A very popular university with fourteen schools of study; some examining done by continuous assessment. 4,000 students; 60% of first years can be accommodated on or near campus. Sports facilities adjacent to campus. (*The University of Bath, Claverton Down, Bath BA2 7AY. Tel 0225 826826*) UCCA.

Bedford (CHE): 750 students in a college in pleasant surroundings. Long tradition in primary teaching and sport. Modular studies available. (*Bedford College of Higher Education, 37 Lansdowne Road, Bedford MK40 2BZ. Tel 0234 351966*) PCAS.

Belfast (Univ): Site to the south of city. Nine subject faculties. Equal balance between arts and science students. 8,400 students, about half of whom live at home, and 29% in university accommodation. (*The University of Belfast, University Road, Belfast BT7 1NN, Northern Ireland. Tel 0232 245133*) UCCA.

Birmingham (Poly): 6,500 full-time students. Main campus 2 miles from the city. Other campuses for art, music and teacher training. (*City of Birmingham Polytechnic, Perry Bar, Birmingham B42 2SU. Tel 021 331 5000*) PCAS.

Birmingham (Univ): Edgbaston site, 2.5 miles from city. A fairly popular university with 10,000 students; accommodation for more than 50%. Wide range of subjects. Five faculties, largest being science and engineering. ('A modern campus, plenty of green areas. Take a bike.') (*The University of Birmingham, PO Box 363, Birmingham B15 2TT. Tel 021 414 3344*) UCCA.

Bishop Grossteste (Coll): 1,600 students. The college offers courses leading to BEd degrees of Hull University. All students spend their second year at the university. (*Bishop Grossteste College, Newport, Lincoln LN1 3DT. Tel 0522 527347*) UCCA.

Bolton (IHE): 2,200 full-time and sandwich students follow a wide range of courses. (*Bolton Institute of Higher Education, Deane Road, Bolton BL3 5AB. Tel 0204 28851*) PCAS.

Bournemouth (Poly): Two sites. 5,642 students. Accommodation for all students either on campus or in lodgings. (*Bournemouth Polytechnic, Dorset House, Talbot Campus, Fern Barrow, Dorset BH12 5BB. Tel 0202 524111*) PCAS.

Bradford (Univ): City-centre site for the three Boards of Studies. 5,000 students divided between engineering, natural and applied sciences and social sciences. 40% of students not living at home are housed in university accommodation. (*The University, Bradford, West Yorkshire BD7 1DP. Tel 0274 733466*) UCCA.

Bradford and Ilkley (CmC): A very large college with 3,600 students full-time following Bradford University BA and BEd degree courses. (*Bradford and Ilkley Community College, Great Horton Road, Bradford, West Yorkshire BD7 1AY. Tel 0274 753026*) UCCA.

Bretton Hall (Coll): The college is located in 250 acres of attractive parkland. 350 students follow art, dance, drama and music courses for which it is famous, along with other courses. Leeds University degrees. (*Bretton Hall College, West Bretton, Wakefield, West Yorkshire WF4 4LG. Tel 0924 830261*) UCCA.

Brighton (Poly): Four sites with one at Eastbourne for those studying sport, science, hotel and catering, teaching or chiropody. 6,500 students. (*Brighton Polytechnic, Lewes Road, Brighton BN2 4AT. Tel 0273 600900*)

Bristol (Poly): A popular institution with five sites. 6,700 students. (*Bristol Polytechnic, Coldharbour Lane, Frenchay, Bristol BS16 1QY. Tel 0272 656261 - Admissions 0272 653221*) PCAS.

Bristol (Univ): A very popular university with 8,300 students. Seven faculties. 44% of students in university accommodation. (*The University of Bristol, Senate House, Bristol BS8 1TH. Tel 0272 303030*) UCCA.

Brunel (Univ): Two campuses approximately 15 miles west of London. Faculties of technology, mathematics and science and social science at Uxbridge; faculty of education and design at Runnymede. Four-year 'thin sandwich' courses, with periods of academic study integrated with industrial and professional training. Approximately 3,000 students with accommodation for about 1,700. Good amenities, modern architecture at Uxbridge, traditional Victorian architecture at Runnymede. (*Brunel, The University of West London, Uxbridge, Middlesex UB8 3PH. Tel 0895 274000*) UCCA.

Buckingham (Univ): Independent university in restored historic buildings on the edge of the market town of Buckingham. 750 students and a friendly atmosphere. Pleasant new accommodation mostly on campus. Degrees taken in only two years. (*The University of Buckingham, Hunter Street, Buckingham MK18 1EG. Tel 0280 814080*) UCCA.

Buckinghamshire (CHE): 2,000 full-time students on three campuses offering a wide range of courses. (*Buckinghamshire College of Higher Education, Newland Park, Gorelands Lane, Chalfont St Giles, Buckinghamshire HP8 4AD. Tel 02407 4441*) PCAS.

Camborne (School of Mines): 125 students in a specialist college offering geology, mining and materials science. (*Camborne School of Mines, Trevenson, Pool, Redruth, Cornwall TR15 3SE. Tel 0209 714866*) PCAS.

Cambridge (Univ): Founded in 13th century. 13,500 students, about 37.6% are women. Thirty one colleges dominate the town of 100,000 people. Twenty faculties offering a wide range of subjects. Students admitted by colleges, not to the university. Library of 3,000,000 volumes as well as faculty and departmental libraries. Most students live in colleges or college lodgings. Over 300 societies, and excellent sports facilities. There are three colleges which admit women only (Lucy Cavendish - mature women, New Hall and Newnham) and twenty five which admit both men and women undergraduates. These are Christ's, Churchill, Clare, Corpus Christi, Downing, Emmanuel, Fitzwilliam, Girton, Gonville & Caius, Homerton (BEd only), Jesus, King's, Magdalene, Pembroke, Peterhouse, Queens', Robinson, St Catharine's, St Edmund's (graduates and mature undergraduates), St John's, Selwyn, Sidney Sussex, Trinity, Trinity Hall and Wolfson (graduates and mature undergraduates). (Enquiries should be addressed to the *Tutor for Admissions, ... College, Cambridge,* or to *Cambridge Intercollegiate Applications Office, Tennis Court Road, Cambridge CB2 1QJ. Tel 0223 333308*).

Cardiff (IHE): The Institute has 3,500 full-time students. It is located in six centres within easy reach of the city centre. (*Cardiff Institute of Higher Education, PO Box 377, Llandaff Centre, Western Avenue, Cardiff CF5 2SG. Tel 0222 551111*) PCAS.

Cardiff (Univ): See under Wales (Univ).

Central London (Poly): Fourteen sites. 5,400 students. (*Polytechnic of Central London, 309 Regent Street, London W1R 8AL. Tel 071 911 5000*) PCAS.

Charlotte Mason (Coll): The college offers a BEd degree of Lancaster University. This small college is located in the heart of the Lake District. (*Charlotte Mason College of Education, Ambleside, Cumbria LA22 9BB. Tel 05394 33066*) UCCA.

Cheltenham and Gloucester (CHE): The college is located on five sites and has a student population of 3,000 full-time. (*Cheltenham and Gloucester College of Higher Education, The Park, Cheltenham, Gloucestershire GL50 2RH. Tel 0242 532834*) PCAS.

Chester (Coll): The college has 23 students preparing for the BA, BSc and BEd degrees of Liverpool University. (*Chester College, Cheyney Road, Chester CH1 4BJ. Tel 0244 375444*) UCCA.

Christ Church (Coll): The college is situated in the city of Canterbury and has 1,700 full-time students preparing for Kent University degrees. (*Christ Church College, North Holmes Road, Canterbury, Kent CT1 1QU. Tel 0227 762444*) PCAS.

City (Poly): Six sites. 3,700 students. Accommodation for 750. (*City of London Polytechnic, India House, 139 Minories, London EC3N 2EY. Tel 071 283 1030*) PCAS.

City (Univ): The university was established in 1966. Small campus site by the City of London. 3,400 students. Strong emphasis on science and technology. Accommodation for 805 students. (*The City University, Northampton Square, London EC1V OHB. Tel 071 253 4399*) UCCA.

Colchester (Inst): (*Colchester Institute, Sheepen Road, Colchester CO3 3LL. Tel 0206 761660*) PCAS.

Coventry (Poly): A modern, purpose-built institution on a central site in Coventry. 7,000 students. (*Coventry Polytechnic, Priory Street, Coventry CV1 5FB. Tel 0203 631313*) PCAS.

Cranfield (IT): Cranfield is a technological university with 2,000 students, mainly postgraduate. There are two faculties offering undergraduate courses (see below). (*Cranfield Institute of Technology, Bedford MK43 0AL. Tel 0234 750111*) UCCA.

Cranfield (Silsoe College): This is the Faculty of Agricultural Engineering, Food Production and Rural Land Use. (*Silsoe College, Bedford MK45 4DT. Tel 0525 60428*) UCCA.

Cranfield (The Royal Military College of Science at Shrivenham): This faculty of Cranfield comprises schools of electrical engineering and science, mechanical, materials and civil engineering and defence management. (*The Royal Military College of Science, Shrivenham, Swindon, Wiltshire SN6 8LA. Tel 0793 785400/1*) UCCA.

Crewe and Alsager (CHE): Teaching is undertaken on two campuses with some 2,000 full-time students following a wide range of courses. (*Crewe and Alsager College of Higher Education, Crewe Road, Crewe, Cheshire CW1 1DU. Tel 0270 500661*) PCAS.

Dartington (CA): 373 students are following courses in music, theatre and visual performance. (*Dartington College of Arts, Totnes, Devon TQ9 6EJ. Tel 0803 863234*) PCAS.

Derbyshire (CHE): 2,500 students following a range of courses in a large college in and around Derby on three campuses. (*Derbyshire College of Higher Education, Kedleston Road, Derby DE3 1GB. Tel 0332 47181*) PCAS.

Doncaster (Coll): The college offers a Leeds University BEng course in Quarry and Road Surfacing Engineering. (*Doncaster College, High Melton, Doncaster DN5 7SZ. Tel 0709 582427*) UCCA.

Dundee (Univ): The university is located on a city centre precinct site. There are 4,200 students (57% Scottish). Accommodation is available for about half the student population. (*The University, Dundee, Scotland DD1 4HN. Tel 0382 23181; Admissions: ext 4028*) UCCA.

Durham-Tees (Coll): The official name of this college is the Joint University College on Teesside. It was designated in October 1991 and will be located at Stockton-on-Tees. The first 240 students will be admitted in October 1992 to courses in European studies, environmental management, environmental technology and human sciences; degrees will be validated jointly by Durham University and Teesside Polytechnic. (*The Admissions Officer, Durham-Tees College, Old Shire Hall, Durham DH1 3HP. Tel 0642 618020*) UCCA.

Durham (Univ): A very popular university with buildings throughout the city, with students admitted to 12 colleges. Seven subject faculties; 5,600 students all of whom can be accommodated within colleges although 15% (approx) live out. There are 12 colleges and one Society admitting undergraduates. Colleges for men: Grey, Hatfield, St Chads, University. Colleges for women: St Mary's. Mixed colleges: Collingwood, St Aidan's, St Cuthbert's, St Hild/St Bede, St John's, Trevelyn, Van Mildert. (*The University of Durham, Old Shire Hall, Durham DH1 3HP. Tel 091 374 2000*) UCCA.

East Anglia (Univ): Campus site two miles from Norwich. 11 schools of study; 4,600 students of whom 60% are in university accommodation. (*The University of East Anglia, Norwich NR4 7TJ. Tel 0603 56161*) UCCA.

East London (Poly): 5,550 full-time and sandwich students centred on two precincts in Dagenham and Stratford. (*The Polytechnic of East London, Romford Road, London E15 4LZ. Tel 081 590 7722*) PCAS.

Edge Hill (CHE): BA and BSc courses followed by 2,500 students on a large attractive rural campus. (*Edge Hill College of Higher Education, St Helen's Road, Ormskirk, Lancashire L39 4QP. Tel 0695 575171*) UCCA.

Edinburgh (Univ): There are eight subject faculties, seven of which (arts, divinity, law, medicine, music, social science and veterinary medicine) are on city centre sites and one, the science faculty (which includes agriculture and engineering), some 3kms from the city centre. Admission is to a faculty, not to a subject department (Faculty of Science admits to subject groups), and transfer between subjects is usually possible. In addition to faculty and departmental libraries, there is a central library with over 2 million volumes. There are over 140 societies and excellent sports facilities. 11,300 students (over 50% Scottish), with university accommodation for 4,660. (*The University, Old College, South Bridge, Edinburgh EH8 9YL, Scotland. Tel 031 650 4360*) UCCA.

Essex (Univ): The university was established in 1964, two miles east of Colchester. 3,600 students (14% from overseas). Five schools of study - comparative, social, law, mathematical science and engineering. Sports facilities on campus. (*The University of Essex, Wivenhoe Park, Colchester CO4 3SQ. Tel 0206 873666*) UCCA.

Exeter (Univ): A very popular university on a wooded hillside site one mile from city centre. Six subject faculties. 6,000 students, 54% living in halls or flats. (*The Univeristy, Northcote House, The Queen's Drive, Exeter, Devon EX4 4QJ. Tel 0392 263263*) UCCA.

Glasgow (Univ): The university is on a 14 acre site one mile from city centre. There are eight subject faculties and a wide range of subjects. There are 12,000 full-time students (80% Scottish; 50% live at home). (*The University, Glasgow G12 8QQ, Scotland. Tel 041 339 8855*) UCCA.

Gwent (CHE): 6,000 full-time and part-time students following courses in art and design, education, management and technology. (*Gwent College of Higher Education, College Crescent, Caerleon, Newport, Gwent NP6 1XJ. Tel 0633 251525*) PCAS.

Hatfield (Poly): 9,500 students. Accommodation for 1,600. Full-time and sandwich students based on three campuses. (*Hatfield Polytechnic, College Lane, Hatfield, Herts AL10 9AB. Tel 0707 279800*) PCAS.

Heriot-Watt (Univ): Founded in 1966 and based on the Riccarton Campus situated 6.5 miles west of central Edinburgh on an attractive 370 acre site of wooded parkland with a small loch. There are five subject faculties: science, engineering, economic and social studies and (in conjunction with Edinburgh College of Art) environmental studies and art and design with 5,300 students in total (approx 60% Scottish). (*Heriot-Watt University, Riccarton, Edinburgh EH14 4AS, Scotland. Tel 031 449 5111*). UCCA.

Holborn (Coll): Law and management courses leading to London (Univ) external (full-time) degrees - and from 1992 Wolverhampton (Poly) law courses. 650 full-time and over 1,000 distance learning students. Internal LLB (CNAA) in conjunction with Wolverhampton Polytechnic. (*Holborn College, 200 Greyhound Road, London W14 9RY. Tel 071 385 3377*) DIRECT.

Homerton (Coll): An approved society of Cambridge University with 690 students. It offers a Bachelor of Education degree only. (*Homerton College, Hills Road, Cambridge. Tel 0223 245931*) UCCA.

Huddersfield (Poly): 5,800 students based on two sites in and near Huddersfield. (*The Polytechnic, Queensgate, Huddersfield HD1 3DH. Tel 0484 422288*) PCAS.

Hull (Univ): A popular university on a compact precinct two miles north of Hull. Wide range of subjects available, divided between four faculties. 6,000 students with accommodation for 70%. (*The University, Hull, North Humberside HU6 7RX. Tel 0482 46311*) UCCA.

Humberside (Poly): 8,000 students on two sites in Hull and Grimsby. (*Humberside Polytechnic, Cottingham Road, Hull HU6 7RT. Tel 0482 445005*) PCAS.

Keele (Univ): The university is located on a very attractive open-country campus near the Potteries. About half the students take the 4-year course including the foundation course after which over half change their original course options. Most of the 3,000 students read two honours subjects. Campus accommodation for 90% of students. (*The University of Keele, Staffordshire ST5 5BG. Tel 0782 621111*) UCCA.

Kent (Univ): The university is located on a 300 acre campus overlooking Canterbury. Wide range of academic subjects. 5,000 students of whom 40% live in one of four colleges, while 60% live out. (*The University of Kent at Canterbury, Canterbury, Kent CT2 7NZ. Tel 0227 764000*) UCCA.

King Alfred's (Coll): 1,250 students following BEd, BA and diploma courses on a campus site. (*King Alfred's College, Sparkford Road, Winchester, Hampshire SO22 4NR. Tel 0962 841515*) PCAS.

Kingston (Poly): 6,700 students on four sites in and around Kingston. (*Kingston Polytechnic, Penrhyn Road, Kingston upon Thames, Surrey KT1 2EE. Tel 081 547 2000*) PCAS.

Lancashire (Poly): 6,100 students following a range of courses on a single town centre site. (*Lancashire Polytechnic, Preston PR1 2TQ. Tel 0772 201201*) PCAS.

Lancaster (Univ): A 200 acre campus site with spectacular views, south of Lancaster. Wide range of subjects available in single or combined (two or three) subject schemes. 5,300 students with half being housed in colleges on the campus. (*Lancaster Univeristy, University House, Lancaster LA1 4YW. Tel 0524 65201*) UCCA.

La Sainte Union (CHE): The College offers Southampton (Univ) degrees in education, combined hons (BA), podiatry and theology. (*La Sainte Union College of Higher Education, The Avenue, Southampton, Hampshire SO9 5HB. Tel 0703 228761*) UCCA.

Leeds (Poly): 7,700 students on two campuses in Leeds and Headingly. (*Leeds Polytechnic, Calverley Street, Leeds LS1 3HE. Tel 0532 832600*) PCAS.

Leeds (Univ): An increasingly popular civic university on compact site just north of city centre. Very wide range of subjects taught including the largest number of arts combinations in any university. 12,200 students. (*The University of Leeds, Leeds LS2 9JT. Tel 0532 431751*) UCCA.

Leicester (Poly): 9,300 students mainly based on the city centre campus. 21 halls of residence. (*Leicester Polytechnic, PO Box 143, Leicester LE1 9BH. Tel 0533 551551*) PCAS.

Leicester (Univ): The university is on a compact site with modern buildings one mile south of the city. 6,000 students with accommodation for 70%, 1,300 on an attractive site 3 miles from the university. (*The University of Leicester, University Road, Leicester LE1 7RH. Tel 0533 522522*) UCCA.

Liverpool (IHE): 2,500 students on three campuses offering BA, BSc and BEd courses validated by Liverpool University. (*Liverpool Institute of Higher Education, PO Box 6, Stand Park Road, Childwall, Liverpool L16 9JD. Tel 051 737 3000*) UCCA.

Liverpool (Poly): 8,700 students following a range of courses on four sites. (*The Liverpool Polytechnic, 70 Mount Pleasant, Liverpool L3 5UX. Tel 051 207 3581*) PCAS.

Liverpool (Univ): Large urban university on an 85 acre compact site close to city centre. Wide range of subjects over seven faculties. 8,700 students, with accommodation guaranteed for all first year students. (*The University of Liverpool, PO Box 147, Liverpool L69 3BX. Tel 051 794 2000*) UCCA.

67

London (Univ) - Birkbeck: Degree courses for mature   part-rime students. Evening teaching. 3,700 students. A-level offers for places not made. (*Birkbeck College, Malet Street, London WC1E 7HX. Tel 071 631 6561*) DIRECT.

London (Univ) - Courtauld Institute of Art: 200 students specialising in the history of European Art. (*The Courtauld Institute of Art, Somerset House, Strand, London WC2R ORN. Tel 071 873 2645*) UCCA.

London (Univ) - Goldsmiths' College: College based at New Cross, 15 mins rail link with Charing Cross. 3,000 students: 1,200 in college halls and houses. (*Goldsmiths' College, Lewisham Way, London SE14 6NW. Tel 081 692 7171*) UCCA.

London (Univ) - Heythrop College: Small college specialising in theology and philosophy with extensive tutorial teaching, with one of the largest theological libraries in the country. Situated near Oxford Circus; 190 students (including 46 post-graduates), with accommodation in intercollegiate halls. (*Heythrop College, 11-13 Cavendish Square, London W1M 0AN. Tel 071 590 6941*)

London (Univ) - Imperial College of Science, Technology and Medicine: Precinct site in South Kensington; a leading college of science and technology with subject areas including engineering, sciences, mining and metallurgy, and now including St Mary's Hospital Medical School. 5,200 students; 1,400 in college accommodation. (*Imperial College of Science and Technology, South Kensington, London SW7 2AZ. Tel 071 589 5111*) UCCA.

London (Univ) - Jews College: This college offers one degree course in Jewish studies. (*Jews College, Albert Road, London NW4 2SJ. Tel 081 203 6427*) UCCA.

London (Univ) - King's College: 6,900 students. (*King's College, Strand, London WC2R 2LS. Tel 071 836 5454*) UCCA.

London (Univ) - Queen Mary and Westfield College: Two campuses in the Mile End Road and Hampstead. 5,400 students. (*Queen Mary College, Mile End Road, London E1 4NS. Tel 071 975 5555*) UCCA.

London (Univ) - Royal Holloway and Bedford New College: The only London University college on a country campus site. Access to Windsor and Staines, and one hour from London centre. Faculties of science, arts and music. 3,100 students of whom a high proportion can be accommodated in college. ('Very impressive, excellent accommodation.') (*Royal Holloway and Bedford New College, Egham Hill, Egham, Surrey TW20 0EX. Tel 0784 434455*) UCCA.

London (Univ) - Royal Veterinary College: Pre-clinical and para-clinical work takes place at Camden Town; clinical work is done on a 470 acre site at Potters Bar, Middlesex. 380 students. (*Royal Veterinary College, Royal College Street, London NW1 OTU. Tel 071 387 2898; Admissions: ext 391*) UCCA.

London (Univ) - School of Economics and Political Science (LSE): 4,000 students. (*London School of Economics and Political Science, Houghton Street, Aldwych, London WC2A 2AE. Tel 071 405 7686*) UCCA.

London (Univ) - School of Oriental and African Studies (SOAS): 1,800 students specialising in Oriental and African studies. Accommodation in intercollegiate halls. (*The School of Oriental and African Studies, Thornhaugh Street, Russell Square, London WC1M OXG. Tel 071 637 2388*) UCCA.

London (Univ) - School of Pharmacy: 350 students specialising in pharmacy. (*The School of Pharmacy, 29-39 Brunswick Square, London WC1N 1AX. Tel 071 753 5830*) UCCA.

London (Univ) - School of Slavonic and East European Studies (SSEES): The School has a student population of 380. (*The School of Slavonic and East European Studies, Malet Street, London WC1E 7HU. Tel 071 637 4934*) UCCA.

London (Univ) - University College: A student body of 8,000. Six faculties and 43 departments offering a wide range of courses. (*University College, Gower Street, London WC1E 6BT. Tel 071 387 7050*) UCCA.

London (Univ) - Wye College: Located five miles from Ashford, Kent and 60 miles from London. Wye College specialises in science subjects with honours courses in agriculture and horticulture. 650 students. Accommodation for 65% of the students. (*Wye College, Wye, Ashford, Kent TN25 5AH. Tel 0233 812401*) UCCA.

London Medical and Dental Schools:

Charing Cross and Westminster Medical School: 850 students. (*St Dunstan's Road, London W6 8RP. Tel 081 846 7272*) UCCA.

King's College Hospital School of Medicine and Dentistry: 840 students. (*Bessemer Road, London SE5 9PJ. Tel 071 274 6222*) UCCA.

London Hospital Medical College: (Dentistry and Medicine) 1,000 students. (*Turner Street, London E1 2AD. Tel 071 377 7611*) UCCA.

Royal Free Hospital School of Medicine: 550 students. (*Rowland Hill Street, London NW3 2PF. Tel 071 794 0500*) UCCA.

St Bartholomew's Hospital Medical College: (Dentistry and Medicine) 560 students. (*West Smithfield, London EC1A 7BE. Tel 071 982 6000*) UCCA.

St George's Hospital Medical School: 770 students. (*Cranmer Terrace, Tooting, London SW17 0RE. Tel 081 672 9944*) UCCA.

St Mary's Hospital Medical School: 570 students. (*Norfolk Place, Paddington, London W2 1PG. Tel 071 723 1252*) UCCA.

United Medical and Dental Schools of Guy's and St Thomas's Hospitals: (Dentistry and Medicine) 1,400 students. (Two sites: *Guy's Campus, London Bridge, London SE1 9RT; St Thomas's Campus, Lambeth Palace Road, London SE1 7EH. Tel 071 922 8013*) Enquiries to St Thomas's Campus only. UCCA.

University College and Middlesex School of Medicine, University College London: 1,000 students (inc dentistry students). (*Gower Street, London WC1 6JJ. Tel 071 387 7050*) UCCA.

Student accommodationn in medical schools is limited, but University of London intercollegiate halls of residence are also available.

Loughborough (Univ): The university was established in 1966 on a campus to the west of the town and offers a wide range of degree and sandwich courses. 5,700 students with a high proportion (3,500) living in the student village. (*University of Technology, Loughborough, Leicester LE11 3TU. Tel 0509 263171*) UCCA.

Luton (CHE): The college offers degree, professional and diploma courses and a large number of HND courses. (*Luton College of Higher Education, Park Square, Luton, Bedfordshire LU1 3JU. Tel 0582 34111*) PCAS.

Manchester (Poly): Based on six sites in and around the city. 13,000 students. (*Manchester Polytechnic, All Saints, Manchester M15 6BH. Tel 061 247 2000*) PCAS.

Manchester (Univ): A large civic university with 12,600 students (approx). (*The University of Manchester, Manchester M13 9PL. Tel 061 275 2000*) UCCA.

Manchester - The University of Manchester Institute of Science and Technology (UMIST): City centre location. One faculty of 20 departments, scientific and technological, but with an extensive management sciences course and European Studies. 5,000 students, 33% sharing residences with the main university body. (*The University of Manchester Institute of Science and Technology, Manchester M60 1QD. Tel 061 236 3311*) UCCA

Middlesex (Poly): Based on seven sites with 7,900 students. (*Middlesex Polytechnic, Bramley Road, Oakwood, London N14 4XS. Tel 081 368 1299*) PCAS.

Nene (Coll): The college offers a range of BA, BSc, BEd and HND courses. (*Nene College, Moulton Park, Northampton NN2 7AL. Tel 0604 715000*) PCAS.

New College, Durham: (*New College, Framwellgate Moor Centre, Durham DH1 5ES. Tel 091 386 2421*) PCAS.

Newcastle (Poly): An increasingly popular polytechnic on two sites with a student population of over 8,000 (full- and part-time) (*Newcastle upon Tyne Polytechnic, Ellison Place, Newcastle upon Tyne NE1 8ST. Tel 091 232 6002*) PCAS.

Newcastle (Univ):   Precinct in the centre of the city with a variety of courses. Over 9,000 students, 46% housed by the university. (*The University of Newcastle upon Tyne, 6 Kensington Terrace, Newcastle upon Tyne, NE1 7RU. Tel 091 222 6000*) UCCA.

Newman and Westhill (Colls):   The colleges offer BEd courses in the nursery, lower primary and upper primary age ranges. Also a BTheol course. Courses are validated by Birmingham University. (*Newman College, Genners Lane, Bartley Green, Birmingham B32 3NT. Tel 021 476 1181; Westhill College, Weoley Park Road, Selly Oak, Birmingham B29 6LL. Tel 021 472 7245*) UCCA.

North Cheshire (Coll):   The college offers three degree course relating to business studies, leisure and media studies. (*North Cheshire College, Padgate Campus, Fearnhead, Warrington WA2 0DB. Tel 0925 814343*) PCAS.

North East Wales (IHE):   4,500 full-time students following BA, BSc, BEng, BEd and nursing courses. (*North East Wales Institute of Higher Education, Cartrefle, Cefn Road, Wrexham, Clwyd LL13 9NL. Tel 0978 290390*) PCAS.

North London (Poly):   5,300 full-time and sandwich students on three sites in Camden, Islington and Central London. (*The Polytechnic of North London, Holloway Road, London N7 8DB. Tel 071 607 2789*) PCAS.

North Riding (Coll):   The college offers BA and BSc degree courses with qualified teacher status validated by Leeds University. (*North Riding College, Filey Road, Scarborough, North Yorkshire YO11 3AZ. Tel 0723 362392*) UCCA.

Nottingham (Poly):   9,400 full-time and sandwich students. (*Nottingham Polytechnic, Burton Street, Nottingham NG1 4BU. Tel 0602 418418*) PCAS.

Nottingham (Univ):   A very popular university on a campus site in parkland west of the city. Large number of courses. 8,300 student population. 13 halls of residence catering for 3,600 students. (*The University of Nottingham, University Park, Nottingham NG7 2RD. Tel 0602 484848*) UCCA.

Oxford (Poly):   A very popular polytechnic with 5,600 students based on two sites. (*Oxford Polytechnic, Headington, Oxford OX3 0BP. Tel 0865 741111*) PCAS.

Oxford (Univ):   Dating from 12th century. 35 colleges admitting students (14,700): 7 for graduates, 2 for women (graduates or under-graduates), and 26 mixed. 16 faculties offering a wide range of courses. Library (the Bodleian) of over 7 million books and 60,000 manuscripts. Of 13,800 students only 2,100 have to live out. (M) = Men only; (W) = Women only. All other colleges are mixed. Group 1: Brasenose, Christ Church, Jesus, Lincoln, Magdalen, Merton, Oriel, St Hilda's (W), Somerville; Group 2: Balliol, Exeter, Keble, Pembroke, St Anne's, St Edmund Hall, St John's, St Peter's, Wadham; Group 3: Corpus Christi, Hertford, Lady Margaret Hall, New College, Queen's, St Catherine's, St Hugh's, Trinity, University, Worcester. Private Halls: Campion Hall (M), St Benet's Hall (M), Mansfield,

Regent's Park, Greyfriars (M). (Enquiries should be addressed to *The Tutor for ....
Admissions, ... College, Oxford,* or *The Oxford Colleges Admissions Office,
University Offices, Wellington Square, Oxford OX1 2JD. Tel 0865 270207)* UCCA.

Portsmouth (Poly): 7,100 students based on two sites with faculties of
environmental studies, engineering, humanities and social sciences and a business
school. (*Portsmouth Polytechnic, Museum Road, Portsmouth PO1 2QQ. Tel 0705
827681).* PCAS.

Reading (Univ): Situated on a large parkland site south of the town with 5
faculties offering a wide range of subjects. 7,600 students, 3,600 in residence. (*The
University of Reading, PO Box 217, Reading, Berkshire RG6 2AH. Tel 0734
875123)* UCCA.

Ripon and York St John (Coll): The college offers Leeds University degrees
in a very wide range of subjects. (*College of Ripon and York St John, Lord Mayor's
Walk, York YO3 7EX. Tel 0904 656771)* UCCA.

Roehampton (Inst): The institute offers Surrey University degrees across four
colleges - Southlands, Whitelands, Digby Stuart and Froebel Institute. (*Roehampton
Institute, Roehampton Lane, London SW15 5PU. Tel 081 878 8117)* UCCA.

St Andrews (Univ): The university dates back to 1413 but is relatively small in
size. There are 4,000 students (68% in student accommodation) and 40% are Scottish.
(*The University of St Andrews, College Gate, St Andrews, Fife KY16 9AJ.
Tel 0334 76161)* UCCA.

St Mark and St John (Coll): Offers BA and BSc courses of Exeter University.
(*St Mark and St John College, Derriford Road, Plymouth PL6 8BH. Tel 0752
777188)* UCCA.

St Martin's (Coll): The college offers a range of Lancaster University degree
courses for 2,600 students. (*St Martin's College, Lancaster LA1 3JD. Tel 0524
63446)* UCCA.

St Mary's (Coll): The college offers BA and BSc courses awarded by Surrey
University. (*St Mary's College, Strawberry Hill, Twickenham, Middlesex TW1
4SX. Tel 081 892 0051)* UCCA.

Salford (University Coll): The college offers a wide range of courses leading to
professional qualifications. (*Salford College of Technology, Frederick Road, Salford
M6 6PU. Tel 061 736 6541)* PCAS.

Salford (Univ): Campus site near Salford centre. 4,200 students (approx). (*The
University of Salford, Salford M5 4WT. Tel 061 745 5000)* UCCA.

Sheffield (Poly): Four sites. 9,600 students. (*Sheffield City Polytechnic, Pond
Street, Sheffield S1 1WB. Tel 0742 720911)* PCAS.

Sheffield (Univ): Large city university, two main sites. Wide range of subjects. 9,400 students, 44% in university accommodation. (*The University of Sheffield, Western Bank, Sheffield S10 2TN. Tel 0742 768555*) UCCA. Medical School *Tel 0742 766222.*

Southampton (IHE): The institute offers BA and BSc courses validated by Southampton University with a population of 2,000 full-time and 11,000 part-time students. (*Southampton Institute of Higher Education East Park Terrace, Southampton SO9 4WW. Tel 0703 229381*) PCAS.

Southampton (Univ): Landscaped site close to the city centre. A wide range of subjects available. 7,300 students, 48% in nearby university accommodation (inc 20 in a purpose-built hall for the disabled). (*The University of Southampton, Highfield, Southampton SO9 5NH. Tel 0703 595000*) UCCA.

South Bank (Poly): 5,800 students based on five sites, the main campus being Southwark. (*South Bank Polytechnic, Borough Road, London SE1 0AA. Tel 071 928 8989*) PCAS.

South West (Poly): Over 8,000 students based on four sites - the largest higher education institution in the region. (*Polytechnic South West, Drake Circus, Plymouth PL4 8AA. Tel 0752 600600*) PCAS.

Staffordshire (Poly): 6,200 students on sites in Stafford and Stoke on Trent. (*Staffordshire Polytechnic, College Road, Stoke-on-Trent ST4 2DE. Tel 0785 52331*) PCAS.

Stirling (Univ): Stirling is located on a large, scenic campus site 2 miles north of the town. Courses relate to management and social sciences, arts, sciences and education. There are 3,300 full-time students with housing for 2,000 on campus. Emphasis is on breadth and flexibility of degree programmes, organised around an academic session of two 15 week semesters. (*The University of Stirling, Stirling FK9 4LA, Scotland. Tel 0786 73171*) UCCA.

Strathclyde (Univ): The university is situated on a city centre site, and is strong in science, technology and business. There are 8,300 students, 55% living at home, thus a high proportion of others can be housed by the university. (*The University of Strathclyde, 16 Richmond Street, Glasgow G1 1XQ, Scotland. Tel 041 553 4170*) UCCA.

Sunderland (Poly): 5,400 students based on two sites. (*Sunderland Polytechnic, Ryhope Road, Sunderland, Tyne and Wear SR2 7EE. Tel 091 515 2000*) PCAS.

Surrey (Univ): The university is in Guildford on a (hill) site next to the cathedral. Bias towards science and technology, but a good choice of alternative subjects. 3,900 students, 56% housed in university accommodation. (*The University of Surrey, Guildford, Surrey GU2 5XH. Tel 0483 300800*) UCCA.

Sussex (Univ): Campus site north of Brighton. Wide range of courses organised in schools of studies. 4,900 students; 1,850 living on the campus. (*The University of Sussex, Sussex House, Falmer, Brighton BN1 9RH. Tel 0273 678416*) UCCA.

Swansea (IHE) (formerly West Glamorgan (IHE)): The institute offers a range of courses covering BA, BSc, BEng and LLB degrees. (*Swansea Institute of Higher Education, Townhill Road, Swansea SA2 0UT. Tel 0792 203482*) PCAS.

Swansea (Univ): See under Wales (Univ).

Teesside (Poly): 5,000 students based on two sites. (*Teesside Polytechnic, Borough Road, Middlesbrough, Cleveland TS1 3BA. Tel 0642 218121*) PCAS.

Thames (Poly): Based on 7 sites in East London and has over 6,500 students following full-time and sandwich courses. (*Thames Polytechnic, Wellington Street, London SE18 6PF. Tel 081 316 8000/8111*) PCAS.

Trinity and All Saints (Coll): Offers a wide range of courses leading to Leeds University degrees. (*Trinity and All Saints' College, Brownberrie Lane, Horsforth, Leeds LS18 5HD. Tel 0532 584341*) UCCA.

Trinity (Coll): BEd and BA courses in humanities and combined studies. (*Trinity College, Carmarthen, Dyfed, South Wales SA31 3EP. Tel 0267 237971*) PCAS.

Ulster (Univ): Four campuses - Jordanstown, Belfast, Coleraine and Londonderry. 9,100 students. (*The University of Ulster, Coleraine, County Londonderry BT52 1SA, Northern Ireland. Tel 0265 44141*) UCCA.

Wales (Poly): One site. 4,800 full-time and sandwich students. The only polytechnic in Wales. (*Polytechnic of Wales, Pontypridd, Mid-Glamorgan CF37 1DL. Tel 0443 480480*) PCAS.

Wales (Univ) - Aberystwyth: Large hill site overlooking town. Balanced range of subjects. 3,600 students with 66% in university accommodation. ('One of the most "Welsh" universities.') Also the College of Librarianship on nearby campus offering a wide range of joint programmes. 400 students. Accommodation for 200. (*The University of Wales, PO Box 2, Aberystwyth, Dyfed SY23 2AX. Tel 0970 622021*) UCCA.

Wales (Univ) - Bangor: Situated in a small city in an area of outstanding natural beauty and historical interest between the mountains of Snowdonia and the shores of the Menai Strait. Wide range of courses in arts, science (including agriculture, forestry and wood science, marine biology and oceanography), music and theology. Facilities include theatre, new drama studio, sports centre with gymnastics hall, three farms, two research vessels, experimental field station and botanical gardens. 3,500 students with 49% in university accommodation. (*The University College of North Wales, Bangor, Gwynedd LL57 2DG. Tel 0248 351151*) UCCA.

Wales (Univ) - Cardiff: 8,700 students. (*The University of Wales College of Cardiff, PO Box 68, Cardiff CF1 3XA. Tel 0222 874412*) UCCA.

Wales (Univ) - Lampeter: College buildings occupy a large area of the small town. All degree courses in the faculty of arts. 950 students, 25% from Wales. Large proportion of students (80%) in university accommodation. ('Small university - but a strong community spirit.') (*St David's University College, Lampeter, Dyfed SA48 7ED. Tel 0570 422351*) UCCA.

Wales (Univ) - Swansea: Campus site west of ther city. Courses in arts, science, technology and social sciences. 5,300 students with accommodation for 53%. (*University College of Swansea, Singleton Park, Swansea SA2 8PP. Tel 0792 205678*) UCCA.

Wales (Univ) - College of Medicine (UWCM): Shares a 53 acre parkland site in Cardiff with University Hospital. 900 medical, dental and nursing students (40% Welsh) with accommodation for about 300. (*The University of Wales College of Medicine, Heath Park, Cardiff CF4 4XN. Tel 0222 747747*) UCCA.

Warwick (Univ): The university was established in 1964 on a large campus site near Coventry. Social science, arts and science subjects offered to 6,900 students. Accommodation for 3,175 on campus where all students can live for one year. (*The University of Warwick, Coventry CV4 7AL. Tel 0203 523523*). UCCA.

Watford (Coll): (*Watford College, Hempstead Road, Watford, Hertfordshire WD1 3EZ. Tel 0923 57500*) PCAS.

West London (IHE): Offers BA, BSc and BEd courses with 2,750 students on two campuses to the west of London. (*West London Institute of Higher Education, 300 St Margarets Road, Twickenham, Middlesex TW1 1FT. Tel 081 891 0121*) PCAS.

West London (Poly) (formerly Ealing College, London and Thames Valley College): (*Polytechnic of West London, St Mary's Road, London W5 5RF. Tel 081 579 5000*) PCAS.

Westminster (Coll): The college has a long tradition of teacher training courses. 750 students. (*Westminster College, North Hinksey, Oxford OX2 9AT. Tel 0865 247644*) PCAS.

West Sussex (IHE): The Institute offers BA, BEd and BSc courses. 1,900 students based on two sites at Bognor Regis and Chichester. (*West Sussex Institute of Higher Education, Upper Bognor Road, Bognor Regis, West Sussex PO21 1HR. Tel 0243 865581*) PCAS.

Wolverhampton (Poly): Five campuses with a population of 7,100 full-time and sandwich students. (*Wolverhampton Polytechnic, Wulfruna Street, Wolverhampton WV1 1SB. Tel 0902 313000*) PCAS.

Worcester (CHE): Offers a range of degree courses including education and combined studies. (*Worcester College of Higher Education, Henwick Grove, Worcester WR2 6AJ. Tel 0905 748080*) PCAS.

York (Univ): Founded in 1963 the university is situated on a beautiful campus east of the city. Arts, natural sciences and social science courses. 4,300 students, each being a member of a college. Majority live in college for first year. (*The University of York, Heslington, York YO1 5DD. Tel 0904 430000*) UCCA.

PUBLICATIONS ORDER FORM

Please enter details of the publications you wish to purchase. Detach the page and send it to us with the appropriate remittance. Please remember to add the relevent amount for postage and packing.

Please insert your full name below:

Address:

Date of order:

TITLE	QUANTITY	PRICE
'The Way In' - Degree and Diploma Courses (£5.95 + 50p p&p per copy)		
'The Way In' - A Career In Law (£5.95 + 50p p&p per copy)		
'The Way In' - After 'A' Level Results: Changing Direction (£5.95 + 50p p&p per copy)		
'The Way In' - Business and Management Courses (£5.95 + 50p p&p per copy)		
'The Way In' - A Career in Accountancy (£5.95 + 50p p&p per copy)		
TOTAL BOOK PRICE		

Please ensure that you enclose a cheque or draft payable to **THE HLT GROUP LTD** for the above amount, or charge to ❑ **Access** ❑ **Visa** ❑ **American Express**

Card Number

Expiry Date .... Signature ....

The Higher Education Advice and Planning Service, a part of the HLT Group, is an Independant advisory service for schools and corporate bodies on career planning and entry to UK higher education. For details of the services provided, please contact: Mr Brian Heap, Director, Higher Education Advice and Planning Service, 200 Greyhound Road, London W14 9RY. Telephone: 071 385 3377 Fax: 071 381 3377